WORLDS within WORDS

Also by Sharon Darrow

Old Thunder and Miss Raney

The Painters of Lexieville

Through the Tempests Dark and Wild: A Story of Mary Shelley, Creator of Frankenstein

Trash

Yafi's Family: An Ethiopian Boy's Journey of Love, Loss, and Adoption (co-author, Linda Pettitt)

WORLDS within WORDS

Writing and the Writing Life

SHARON DARROW

Pudding Hill Press

Sutton, Vermont

Copyright © 2018 by Sharon Darrow

All rights reserved. No part of this publication may be reproduced, distributed or transmitted in any form or by any means, without prior written permission.

Pudding Hill Press
5463 Pudding Hill
Sutton, Vermont 05867
www.sharondarrow.com

Worlds within Words: Writing and the Writing Life/ Sharon Darrow. -- 1st ed.
ISBN 978-0-9986878-0-3

In celebration of the Twentieth Anniversary (2017) of the first Master of Fine Arts program dedicated to creating literature for young people, the MFA in Writing for Children & Young Adults, Vermont College of Fine Arts.

Dedicated with love and gratitude to the students, alumni, faculty, and staff of VCFA

ACKNOWLEDGMENTS

First of all, thank you to my colleagues on the faculty of the MFA in Writing for Children & Young Adults, Vermont College of Fine Arts.

Founding faculty: Marion Dane Bauer, Jack Gantos, Chris Lynch, Graham Salisbury, Jacqueline Woodson, and Louise Hawes.

Current faculty: Tim Wynne-Jones, Martine Leavitt, Jane Kurtz, Margaret Bechard, A. M. Jenkins, Alan Cumyn, Uma Krishnaswami, Cynthia Leitich Smith, Mary Quattlebaum, A. S. King, Shelley Tanaka, Tom Birdseye, An Na, David Gill, Kekla Magoon, Will Alexander, Linda Urban, Nova Ren Suma, Liz Garton Scanlon, Varian Johnson, and Martha Brockenbrough.

Former faculty: Brock Cole, Bruce Brooks, Ellen Howard, Jane Resh Thomas, Phyllis Root, Susan Fletcher, Liza Ketchum, Mark Karlins, Chris Raschka, Randy Powell, Lisa Jahn-Clough, Carolyn Coman, Ron Koertge, Adam Rapp, Amy Ehrlich, Mel Glenn, M. T. Anderson, David Gifaldi, Elizabeth Partridge, Laura McGee Kvasnovsky, Kathi Appelt, Eric Kimmel, Alison McGhee, Deborah Wiles, Leda Schubert, Franny Billingsley, Brent Hartinger, Paul Janeczko, Marc Aronson, Julie Larios, Rita Williams-Garcia, Sarah Ellis, Garret Freymann-Wehr, Coe Booth, Matt de la Peña, April Lurie, and Daniel José Older.

Administration & Staff: Louise Crowley, Melissa Fisher, Kate Gustafson, Vicki Wasley, Aidan Samis, Ann Cardinal, Bill

Kaplan, Thomas Christopher Greene, Roger Weingarten, and so many others.

In memoriam: Craig Crist-Evans, Ellen Levine, Norma Fox Mazer, and Bonnie Christensen.

I am grateful to my teachers, friends, editors, and mentors: Lynn Sloan (especially on this project for her encouragement and invaluable editorial and book design advice), Stephen O. Harmon, Fred Shafer, Brett Lott, David Wojahn, David Jauss, Sidney Lea, Phyllis Barber, Mary Peterson Clyde, Rebekah Boyd, Scott Withiam, Melanie Kroupa, Mary Lee Donovan, Lee Bennett Hopkins, Mary Maloney, Cynthia Brinson, Karen Miller, Esther Hershenhorn, Sharon Sloan Fiffer, Laura Ruby, Carolyn Crimi, Esme Codell, Myra Sanderman, Erzsi Deak, Sharon Solwitz, Barry Silesky, Becky Bradway, Sue Anzaldi, Columbia College Chicago, Paul Hoover, Jean Naggar Agency, Barry Goldblatt, Jo Knowles, Cynthia Faughnan, Nicole Griffin, Daphne Kalmar, Dana Walrath, Cheryl Klein, Beth Bacon, Marianne Murphy—to name only a few. Also, gratitude to the members of Fred Shafer's Short Story and Novel Workshops, Off-Campus Writers, The Writers (Chicago), and The Society of Children's Book Writers and Illustrators.

Thank you to VCFA's MFA-C&YA alumni, and to those who have come back as graduate assistants in our residencies. We couldn't run a residency without you. A special thank you to those of you who have been my students for all you have taught me. I am so grateful for our alumni's dedication, courage, and support and love for one another. The VCFA community of artists is unique, strong, and beautiful, and I am so proud and humbled to be a part of it.

Overflowing love and gratitude to my daughters, Kristen, Elizabeth, and Stephanie, and their families for their unfailing support and belief in me, as well as Kristen's editorial expertise; to my stepsons, Harper and Owain, and their families for their acceptance and encouragement; to my mother, my sister Nancy, and her husband Jeff, and my nieces and nephews for support and understanding; and to my husband Jerry Clyde Phillips, editor *extraordinaire*, for his kindness, love, and, especially, his partnership and hard work to make this book a reality.

CONTENTS

INTRODUCTION..1

PART I: THE WRITING LIFE

THE CLOTHESLINE: PLACE AND IDENTITY..........9

   Exercise: Remembering an Earlier Time and Place....24

VOICE, INSPIRATION, AND MEANING..................25

   Exercise: Voice Lessons 46

PORTALS AND NEGATIVE SPACE.........................47

    I. PORTALS..47

    II. NEGATIVE CAPABILITY AND NEGATIVE SPACE 51

    III. WHERE STORY LIVES 56

   Exercise: Negative Capability......................................57

PART II: THE CRAFT AND THE ART

CHARACTERIZATION:
CHOOSING POINT OF VIEW......................................61

   Exercise: Practice in Point of View 83

EMOTION AND REVSION:
THE "EMOTIONAL CORE"..85

   Exercise: Statement and Evocation............................110

TWO SIDES OF THE SAME COIN: CHARACTER'S EMOTIONAL JOURNEY AND THE PLOT 113

   Exercise: Exploring Emotion Over Time..................130

THE PLOT OF THE SENTENCE:
SOME TACTICS OF SYNTAX 133
    Exercise: Re-plotting Sentences 149
POETRY: "A MESSY BUSINESS".......................... 151
    Exercise: Poetry 163

PART III: THE TEACHING WRITER
TEACHING: THE PROCESS APPROACH TO
WRITING 167
    Exercise: Dialogue with Texts, Other Writers........... 181
THE WRITING AND TEACHING LIFE.................... 183
    Exercise: Saving Lives, Changing Worlds 195
"WRITE AT YOUR OWN RISK" EXCERPTS AND
OTHER SHORT PIECES 197
    Discovering YOUR Stories 198
    Metaphorical Thinking 201
    Action and Reflection 204
    A Room of My Own……………………………………..206
    Here Be Dragons: Placing the Story………………….210
    Family Life and Writing…………………………………214
    S.W.E.P.T.: Making a Clean Sweep.......................... 217
    Sharon's Top Five Writing Mistakes......................... 224

PART IV: IMAGINATION, REVISION, AND SELF-
MAKING
WHAT DO YOU THINK YOU ARE DOING?.......... 227
    Exercise: Developing Your Writer's Statement 252

DISCOVERING THE REAL STORY 253

PART V: GOING FORWARD
RISKS TO BE TAKEN; DREAMS TO BE DREAMED
(A Graduation Address) 259
    NOTES ON THE ESSAYS 275
    ABOUT THE AUTHOR……………………….....281

INTRODUCTION

We are writers on a wonderful journey, some just setting out, others farther along the path, but we all are striving to live the best writing lives possible. As I've traveled from learner to teacher, from unpublished explorer to published author, I've often asked myself questions about my purpose and effectiveness, questions that I want to pose to you in this book: What do you think you are doing? And why? How can you live your life to the fullest? What are your hopes, dreams, and fears? How are your deepest needs and deepest self connected to your choice of art and career? What do you need to learn and practice to become a writer who not only strives for excellence, but also achieves it? What are you trying to say to readers and to yourself? Do you even know? What happens when things don't turn out as you plan? How do you persist through life's (and the market's) ups and downs? These are questions that I believe writers must ask themselves as they proceed through their writing lives, questions to be asked and answered many times over the course of their careers in writing.

I have had ideas about objectives, goals, and purpose on my mind about my own life for many years, as every writer does, whether just beginning the writing journey or already somewhere along it. I'd like to challenge you to pause on your path now and spend some time thinking about what it is to feel a sense of purpose beyond one's self, to know that you are meant to do something—and then to do it. Isn't that what life is about, what life is for? Purpose—and along with it happiness, fulfillment, and joy?

For humans, the pursuit of happiness, fulfillment, and joy often revolves around issues of how we spend our time, what jobs we accomplish and activities we choose, our relationships with family and friends, and our ability to live our lives honestly with others and with ourselves. As we learn and grow we endeavor to develop mature selves through the exercise of responsibility to others *and to ourselves*. How often have we, in our attempts to fulfill outside expectations, forgotten that living responsibly has two parts, both in relationship to others and to ourselves? How can we follow more of our own inner urgings to live effectively in the world through engagement with the written word while still fulfilling our other roles, and how can we bring these aspects of our lives into balance?

For many of us, the choice of a writing life is the way in which we honestly answer our inner need for purpose and how we encounter the world outside ourselves with integrity. Because I believe this choice and the questions that come with it to be of great important to each of us, I offer some of my ideas in the following chapters. In hearing about some of my challenges, experiences, successes, and some of the things I've learned and shared with my students, I hope you will be inspired to spend some time examining how your writing life has gone, is going, and where you want it to go.

With mere words on paper, writers create new worlds on the page, new adventures for readers to encounter, worlds rich with emotion and action, dreams and magic, stories that enthrall and empower. The process of imagination forged into story through the amazing facility language allows has changed the lives of both writers and readers. For those of us who have been fortunate enough to be associated with the MFA in Writing programs of Vermont College of Fine Arts, our own worlds have grown richer and more empowered through the ways learning about and using language has shaped us. As the MFA in Writing for Children and Young Adults program reached its Twentieth Anniversary, I was reminded of all the college has meant to me and has done for me. I am honored to have had the opportunity to study writing there in the original MFA-Writing program, and to become an advisor of other writers in the MFA-Writing for Children & Young Adults program, its younger sister.

When I was a student, the MFA in Writing inspired me to add the study and writing of poetry to my work in prose. Poetry has enriched my fiction and given me another mode of thought and expression, one that has enhanced the whole of my life as a writer, teacher, and person. That study gave me a foundation for teaching, something I had never planned to do. Now, having taught at VCFA for twenty years, I've had the opportunity to examine what I think, know, and believe about writing and about teaching. In this volume I've gathered a few essays gleaned from lectures that I have had the joy of presenting in our Writing for Children and Young Adult residencies over the years.

I've chosen essays to include that speak to the writing life and how one's writing and one's life each impinge upon and transform the other. In these essays, I consider place and identity, voice and memory, as well as portals and negative space as they apply to imagination and the idea of "negative capability' or the ability to "dwell in uncertainty." In the section on the craft and the art of writing, I share a few of my notions about more technical aspects of characterization, emotion, revision, poetry, and sentence making. With the section on the teaching writer, I lean upon the writings of pedagogical philosophers and teachers, Paulo Freire, Peter Elbow, and Nancy Atwell, whose ideas and ideals have inspired me and buoyed me through my teaching career.

In addition, I've included some of my shorter pieces and excerpts from our MFA-WCYA faculty blog *Write at your Own Risk*. These might come under the heading "This Writer's Life," and are personal reflections of what this writing life has meant for me and to me.

I end with a section on developing your own Writer's Statement, with some ideas about how imagination and revision are causes of and effects on the growth of the self, and a chapter adapted from the graduation addresses I delivered in January 2007 and January 2017.

I hope that these essays will inspire you to a stronger belief in yourself as a writer and will spur you on to the creation of many new characters and stories. Maybe they will also give you a little taste of Vermont College of Fine Arts whether you have been there to experience it for yourself in the camaraderie of the green and sunny days of summer and the snug coziness of the icy snow-covered winter residencies, or have looked on from afar. Whether near or far, we are writers whose primary concerns have been to write for and about young people. I believe this to be a noble calling and one that has the power to save lives and change the world, one reader at a time.

SD

PART I

THE WRITING LIFE

CHAPTER ONE

THE CLOTHESLINE: PLACE AND IDENTITY

When I entered Vermont College to study writing, I realized revision of my work would involve changing and rearranging words on the page. It would require thinking about my stories and plotting and planning in ways I had not yet encountered. I didn't yet know that it would also necessarily bring about other deeper changes, changes in self and in identity. I didn't know that coming to Vermont College would help me become not just the writer I needed to become in order to write what I needed to write, but the kind of person I needed to become to do so. Of course, I had an inkling that the changes would be significant, that I would learn a lot, hone my skills, meet new people, but I didn't yet know that by changing one word at a time I would also be making tiny incremental changes in myself as a person. The process of discovery and revision not only changes the words on the page, but also the writer who writes them. The writing process is a process of becoming, a process of transformation. We revise ourselves as we revise our words. And as we revise our words and ourselves, we revise our worlds.

Some years ago I received from a family member one of those forwarded chain-letter emails, which at the time tended to fill up the inbox and annoy me. Most of them were vaguely veiled threats that if I didn't forward on a dire health warning, a badly rhyming prayer, or a caution about spam or terrorism to at least ten of my closest friends and dear family members, I'd suffer some well-deserved fate for not being responsible enough, religious or patriotic enough to keep someone else's idea of the truth going across the world wide web. Each time one of these email forwards appeared in my inbox, I was grateful to my mother for not allowing my sister and me to send on the chain letters that came in the postal mail back when I was a child. She told us they were scams and illegal, especially if they asked us to send a penny to the first name on the list and then sit back and wait for a fortune of pennies to land in our mailbox, one at a time. Ah, what a dream come true that would have been for a nine-year-old comic book collector during an idyllic El Paso summer! Still, responding to those letters was forbidden.

Later, I smiled at my mother's own forwarded emails because she usually sent me a little note with them: "You don't need to forward this on, but I thought you'd like it." Sometimes I wondered if she, herself, had succumbed to these anonymous intimations that she might be somehow letting God down if she didn't send on the messages—or letting her children down, she who still felt responsible for our safety and our religious instruction even though she was nearly ninety years old and had great-grandchildren at her feet.

It's funny now how easily those emails could stir up the emotions—either making me laugh out loud and feel good or cringe and feel guilty or feel bad for disliking the art that accompanied them or confront my superstitions with a kind of chagrin when I did, in fact, send them on.

When I received this particular chain-letter email about war and terrorism, I had been researching the background of the medieval period's wars between Christians and Muslims and the Inquisition against heretics and Jews. Because of this disheartening research, coupled with my own feelings about war, I asked my family member to stop sending me such forwards, most of which seemed to echo those faraway prejudices from long ago. After that, no forwarded messages from her appeared in my inbox until about six months later when "The Clothesline" arrived. That turned out to be the same day she sent my mother a prayer about counting your blessings, a prayer that my mother forwarded on to me a few hours later. I suppose she had decided that I was not interested in wars and prayers, but would like to be included in a sentimental walk down memory lane about hanging out the clothes.

Actually, I *was* interested in reading about what the article called the "lost art" of clothes hanging, the sunny day breezes through the freshly washed linens, the stiff-legged rattle of our fathers' frozen khaki work pants on a frosty winter day, the way each item has its correct hanging method (pants upright, shirts upside down by their tails, sheets and towels on the outer lines, unmentionables inside to hide them). I was most struck, surprised even, by the tone of finality over the passing of an historic time and a quaint womanly duty. Why? Because in my life clothes hanging wasn't lost. To this day it's one of my favorite tasks during the warm time of year. I start hanging out the clothes just as soon as the rain stops and the sun shines in Vermont and keep on till the fallen leaves have icy crusts that crackle under my feet. I love hanging out those wet clothes on a hot day, my shoulders growing damp from the towels piled on them as I move down the row, digging the pins from a basket hung on my arm, the weathered wood of the clothespins rough and warm in my pinching fingers. Later, I love pulling the heated and air-scented clothes into my arms and dropping the pins back into the basket at my feet, seeing how many hit square on and how many bounce out to be retrieved later, then folding the dry clothes, those stiff towels promising the good rough memory of these sunny moments when I towel myself dry after a shower before bed. I love the connection to my past, my family, even those memories of my little freezing fingers trying to unpin a frozen shirt from the line when I was eleven in Oklahoma City or the way the hot metal hinge stung after hours in the deep south Texas sun blaze. I actually like having to run outdoors to grab half-dry clothes off the line as the wind whips around and a storm comes rolling down over the Green Mountains making me remember how the sudden Blue Northers of my childhood marched in over the horizon on the Great Plains, the emergency of saving the wet clothes from the advancing dust storm, and the first huge and dirty rain-scented drops.

What is lovely right now, here in another millennium, the twenty-first century, is the connection I feel to my new home and the neighbors all around me in Vermont who are also hanging out their clothes, or are, even as I rush into the blowing rain, rushing with me all over the county, laughing into the storm. Now, almost everyone I know has a clothesline and, what's more, uses it. Maybe they have continued all these years and never given into the lure of the clothes dryer, or maybe they now aim to use less electricity and oil. I'm not sure because this isn't my home region and I don't really know the folkways. I just know it feels great to have some common ground in the summerland of Vermont rural life. It brings me home, here in New England, so far from my original Southern roots.

Then, when I'm sitting on my large front porch, the rain dripping off the roof around me, enclosing me in my own writing space, I can allow my fingers to dance over the keys on my laptop, and allow my heart and mind to go into story. These stories are born of the self I've been, the self I am, and the self I am becoming each day through the small moments as well as the large, but maybe most of all the self I am able to be and become through my own stories. Being a writer isn't one special moment of achievement—the diploma, the finished thesis, the first published piece, the reading, the school visit, the class taught, the starred review, the acclaim, the prize or award. It's not one large moment, but many small moments of just being, and allowing yourself to honor your experiences, no matter how small, and, perhaps, allow them to find their way into your stories and poems. It's writing from the imagination and the self, allowing both to be honored equally; it's finding our own truths through the imagining of what might be here in this world of today, but often in worlds never before seen and through people never born except in the miraculous imagination of our own hearts and minds.

In my teaching, I'm always talking about getting to the heart of things, bringing the deepest reaches of the human heart to the page through the embodiment of sensation and emotion in our characters. I want to detect the heartbeat on my fingertips through the page, shiver with the breath of danger down my neck, and taste the salt of sweat or tears on my tongue. At the first scent of rain in the air, I want my characters to spring from their chairs laughing, feet slipping into their flip-flops at the door, screen doors banging behind them, clomp of the porch boards underfoot, splash of the first cold raindrops against their heated faces, as they rush to bring in the wash from the line. I want to be there at the clothesline with them, to experience the emotions they bring into that moment from the last phone call with a sick grandparent on her death bed, or the smile of a little brother just falling asleep for an afternoon nap, or the stresses of school, social life, or a parent who drinks too much. I want to discover "what happens" in the character's life, by asking "What if this and what if that?" I want to allow the plot to unfold from the inciting situation through the inner responses of the character, the "Why?" behind how a character responds to a situation, and continue through the next development and the next. The plot of a story moves through logical steps from beginning through complicating middle to the satisfying end, but these steps will be different depending upon who the character is and upon what that particular character will do to seek equilibrium in her life by striving to solve her own problem despite obstacle after obstacle rising before her.

    I suspect you've heard the general rules of thumb over and over again that go something like this: In order to develop a story, you need to have a character who has a problem, who seeks to solve that problem, failing through successive tries, until at the last gasp, the character gives one final supreme effort that will either succeed or fail and thus end the story through a resolution, one that is surprising and yet satisfying and in some way inevitable. Usually, the character experiences insight, an epiphany, and becomes able to move on in a new or at least altered direction. A story or novel ends where it does because it projects the next life path of the character and, in effect, tells us all we need to know about that character for us to understand where he is headed in the future, therefore needing no further development through story. The difference between a short story and a novel has to do in great part with time elapsed in the tale and how much has to be shown in order to deliver the character from the entry point and the problem associated with it to a new level of being in the world that will persist for some time, even if for a short time, as may be the case when we are dealing with children and teenagers as characters.

Stories are pretty much made up of the same expectations and movements, so wherein do their differences lie? Well, in situation, character, event, and outcome. And where do those arise? In the one-of-a-kind self of the author. We are all unique because of our own individual experiences; our familial, genetic, and societal backgrounds; the geographies we've experienced through travel or residence; and a myriad other factors. We have different original languages or dialects and accents. We have different wells of emotion and different reasons for coming to writing as the art of our life's expression. Each of these things affects how we make our stories, how we experience our characters, and how we choose the diction, tone, and voice of the pieces we write. All of this, taken together, determines the kind of philosophy we project onto our stories, the conscious or unconscious "lessons" brought out through the telling of the tale, and, not least, the motivation behind our writing, the reasons we come to writing in the first place.

Have you thought deeply about why you write? Why do you write for your chosen audience, whether adults or children or teenagers? What do you write for yourself? Have you set out to reprimand, instruct, proselytize, judge, cajole, save, or scare readers into changing their lives? If so, why? Are you sure you have all the answers yourself?

An honest writer doesn't write to teach a moral lesson, but comes to the problem with an open mind. We write to discover what we think or believe, and then, if we are lucky, to share some new and hard-won wisdom through story. We write to allow readers to live vicariously through experiences we would never wish on them in real life. In order to do that, we have to stop protecting our characters. We have to let all manner of evil, mischief, or sorrow fall upon their heads. If we are writing for young people, we have to deny our innermost needs and best meant wishes for real children and allow our fictional character-children to suffer and rage, be afflicted, abused, or made heartsick with despair. Sometimes the best hope one can give readers is through allowing the character to experience a dearth of hope through calamity and tragedy, to allow our stories to reflect life as it is for many of our readers. We can do this whether we write realistic contemporary stories, or fantasy, science fiction, historical fiction, or what-have-you. Through these stories we let our readers know that they are not alone, despite the conditions of their lives, and that someone understands and cares. By bringing characters to life in circumstances that show and elicit empathy, we build a better world for our readers. And yes, that is hope.

How can we do this? One way, perhaps, is to spend some time considering who we are as people, why we want to write, and even where we come from, the lands of our origins. I've always advocated the exploration of voice through one's own roots, through family story, and regional identity. I hope you will spend time thinking about the turns of phrase, the local prejudices, and the family dynamics that are unique to you and to the place from which you come. But I also hope you will consider how your upbringing, your religious affiliation or non-affiliation, your other spiritual influences, your region's traditions, expectations, flaws, and history vis-à-vis the rest of America and the world has an influence upon how you experience even your smallest moments, and how you allow your characters to experience theirs. Are you controlling your character or do you allow for discovery? Is the outlined plot the thing or is the meandering path your character discovers step by step the way you find your story? Do you rein in emotion or go for the jugular? Do you allow your characters to feel failure or do you try hard to save them from pain? Are you willing to go with the characters on their emotional journeys, thus allowing your own fictions to lead you into new real-life insights and your own true epiphanies?

So many aspects of your adult self today have been determined by the regions and countries in which you've lived, especially those of your birth and childhood, as well as those of your parents. If you haven't spent some time thinking about how those influences impinge upon your everyday life and upon your attitudes toward readers and story, you might want to think about it. It's not just Southerners, Westerners, or Midwesterners who have strong regional identities, but also Quebecois, Puerto Ricans, New Jersey-ites, Brooklyn-ites, New Englanders, etc. What kinds of stories did you like as a child? Would you expect all children to like them, too? If you are interested in writing for young people, are you trying to keep up with the lives and experiences of children today, especially those for whom you are writing? Do you think you have anything to say to readers? If so, which readers? Nonfiction readers, fiction readers, poetry readers? City children and country children, sheltered children and children from the streets? How about children from cultures different from your own? How do any and all of these elements come out of the places and times in which you were raised? Can viewing your own background honestly and as objectively as possible open the doors of your work to readers from very different backgrounds and experiences? What do you really feel about your readers? Do you like them or disapprove of them and seek to change them? Where does that attitude in you originate? Maybe you like them *and* seek to facilitate growth and change in them. Without imposing one's own attitudes and expectations on our readers, what ways can our stories allow readers to discover the truths of their own lives?

"Who are you? Who am I? Who are we?" I ask these questions of you and of myself. I haven't figured out everything about how the region of my birth affects my decision to write at all, or how it impinges upon my decision to write not only for adults, but also for children and young adults, or how it influences what I end up finding to write. My origin in the South and my life in Texas for so many years might at one time have meant I'd be seen as a Texas writer (which I was thrilled to try to become) or a Southern writer (which I felt I could hardly even aspire to be), but it never occurred to me to imagine myself as a writer without a strong regional identity. It's odd to me now not to be seen as a writer from the South by people in the South because I've lived so long now outside that region, first in Chicago and now in Vermont. I see myself as a regional writer who happens occasionally to write something not all that assignable to the South. I hear my voice as Southern, Texan, though now my Texas family and friends comment that I've lost my accent and say my children sound like "Yankees." It's very weird to live in a place where a cranky neighbor writes me a letter threatening my dog's life with the ten guns he has in his house, who calls me a "flatlander" without his knowing that I've indeed lived in other mountains outside of those called Green, am not afraid of how many guns he has in his house as I've lived where people display them in the back window racks of their pickups just above the baby car seats or keep them tucked near at hand between the seat and door when driving across the rolling prairies alone at night, and I don't intend to be frightened off my little acre where there is plenty of water and good soil if I ever decided I wanted to grow something because of my pioneer stock and family heritage of "standing-by-your-man" homesteading, dirt farming, living in half-dugout soddies, and through tornadoes, hurricanes, wildfires, dust bowls, and digging out frozen beef cattle from drifts as high as houses.

My new millennium self is a hodgepodge of all that I've done, seen, and heard, and every place I've been and lived, as well as all the family stories and lore. But I now have a touch of Paris, France in with that large dose of Paris, Texas. When I was young, despite dreams of seeing the world, I'd never have imagined I'd actually have seen as much of it as I have now.

What places have come into your life? How have those places changed you? Write about them, think about them, ask yourself if you have a character growing there in the soil of one of them, and if so, ask what has just happened to that character? What would happen to a character when transplanted from one of those places to another? Why would that happen? Begin as one does for any story by asking, "What if? What if? What if?" Go to "What then?" And finally, "Why?" Never underestimate the places you can go in your imagination and the depths of knowledge and insight your curiosity about the world can give you. When you open yourself to your own experiences, add to that your vast imagination, and your ability to research and make connections, you will be able to connect with readers of many ages, stages, settings, and backgrounds. I believe that the urge to know, to understand, and to immerse oneself in another's life—in our characters' lives—is powered by curiosity and fulfilled in empathy. In that combination we find wellsprings of energy, even a kind of compulsion and a rich and honorable ambition.

When I first began writing, my energy and drive was powerful, irresistible despite the occasions I did try to resist the call of the stories and poems that poured forth as if a cork had popped out of an artesian well inside me. The well, so long pressurized, exploded and I wrote like a house afire. As colleague Kathi Appelt says, I wrote like "my fingers were on fire." I also wrote with great passion and emotion, like *my heart was afire*.

Nowadays, it's different for me. The well has found a more normal flow and is no longer the new writer's pent up explosive force barely able to be checked. Today, I am working at a slower pace, on work that comes from me and from my heart, my self, but not so apparently near my own regional experience. The voice is not derived from the American South and somehow it's harder to trust and follow its leading. I end up second guessing my choices, my characters, their responses, even deciding that I must do more research to know what the characters would be expected to do in that historical time and in those circumstances. I often stop and ask myself what it is in me that is being served by researching the Middles Ages and, for goodness sake, the Crusades. I've never been interested in all that. Why is the person I am becoming now led to read, study, and write about that geography and that time period? What am I doing?

I don't yet know. So I keep asking: Who am I?

I am from a place and time from which clotheslines have passed, and have become relics of memory to be evoked across the world wide web, fodder for old timers' reminiscences, and I am from a place and time in which clotheslines have become *de rigueur* especially if one is interested in the environment and sustainable living, all the rage in present day Vermont. Hanging out the clothes, an activity (and now a symbol) of my past, present, *and* future. How odd life is.

And so I ask again: Who AM I? Who are you?

Exercise:

Remembering an Earlier Time and Place

1. Can you remember a time when a specific place came alive for you? Shut your eyes and go back there in your memory. Spend a couple of minutes visualizing details of that setting—sights, smells, sounds, voices, sensations and emotions.

2. Make a list of those details, words and/or phrases that come from those memories, say up to twenty or so. Allow bits of dialogue onto the list as your memory serves them up, too.

3. Review the list, arranging into a pattern of some sort, perhaps chronologically or by association. Make a list poem that has a summing up statement at the end, or write a prose poem or paragraph that grows out of the intersection of these words and memories, coupled with the self you are today, and the place you find yourself in today.

4. Come back to this writing in a day or two and see if this exercise has triggered other memories and provoked new stories in your imagination. Know that you are practicing writing from your deepest self when you take time to remember and honor the stuff of your life.

CHAPTER TWO

VOICE, INSPIRATION, AND MEANING

When I consider "voice" in writing, I think about all the voices from the past that make up the memories of my life. Many of those memories flood my mind when I remember my mother's voice singing a lullaby or a hymn, my grandmother's voice telling me a story about my daddy when he was two years old, his delighted smile when she grabbed him off the wagon when my grandpa brought him back from days away with his grandmother while his younger brother was being born at home. Or when the smell of mashed potatoes and gravy brings a rush of emotion and echoes of voices at the farmhouse kitchen table where my uncles used to repeat their tales of learning to drive, of Oklahoma red dirt road bridges washing out, and their cars swerving through mud-rutted detours home under the dark, star-filled nights of their youth. Or the time the two younger boys decided to learn to smoke cigarettes while their parents and older brothers had gone to town and they nearly burned the house down. They rolled their own, hid in the north bedroom and got the match too close to my father's brand new high school graduation suit made of some newly invented synthetic material. A new and highly flammable fabric.

Echoing back from that long-ago farmhouse kitchen table come those voices, that laughter, my grandmother's surprise at learning of some of her sons' escapades for the first time, shaking her head and laughing till she cried.

When you remember the voices of your life where do you begin? Come back with me to my beginning. Come back in memory—my mother's warm, alto voice singing:

Soft as the voice of an angel
Breathing a lesson unheard,
Hope with a gentle persuasion
Whispers her comforting word:

"Wait till the darkness is over;
Wait till the tempest is done;
Hope for the sunshine tomorrow
After the shower is gone."

Whispering Hope
O how welcome thy voice
Making my heart
In its sorrow rejoice.

This old hymn, "Whispering Hope," is about resilience and rejoicing in the face of sorrow. We may begin in joy and return to joy, but in between, we humans give voice to so many other emotions, just as our characters must do. We, and they, grasp at the "gentle persuasion" of hope for all our futures.

My earliest memories are filled with voiced stories: Bible stories, moral tales and fables, fairy tales, ghost stories, the funny papers, Golden Books, lullabies, hymns, family remembrances that made the grandmothers laugh till they cried, the men guffaw or do their "aw shucks" thing, and the kids squeal and bounce for joy in the dining room chairs, or hush so as not to be noticed if the subject matter turned serious or began to explain puzzles of kinship, or tread upon the territory of the secret, the sexual, or the romantic.

Startled, stymied, surprised, shocked, or just for emphasis, my family members might say, "Oh, pshaw!" "Fiddle!"—or one of its variations, "Fiddle-dee-dee" or "Fiddlesticks"—"Dad gum," "I swaneeee," "Great sakes alive," "Good heavenly days," "Well, hallelujah," "Good gravy," "Dad-blamed," "I declare to goodness," "My foot!" "My eye!" and so on.

I remember trying to figure out (which I guess is itself another regional idiom) what some of these sayings had to do with what I'd seen or heard. I still remember visiting my grandparents on their farm and trying to combine "good gravy" with something that had just gone wrong in the chicken yard or imagining what a fiddlestick was in the first place, then trying to relate the bow of a violin to the dropped plate of biscuits the dog was now feasting on, or why a mouse glimpsed running across the darkened living room could call forth my usually calm Grandma Darrow's exclamation: "Good Heavenly Days! Floyd, get the broom!"

Later on, I got accustomed to these things and learned how other families spoke. Even though I had heard odd and foreign voices from all over the U.S. and on television, my own idiomatic speech seemed normal and ordinary. That is, until I left Texas and moved to the Chicago area. I heard my voice cut through the department store aisles and saw it turn heads in my direction when I scolded my two younger children for climbing into the center of a circular clothing rack and whirling it around as if a ghostly presence was active in the Kmart, "Y'all git outta there!" I reached in and dragged them out, sweet innocent little curly-haired dolls and the other customers stared agape as if I were going to haul off and tear up my little darlins' backsides right then and there.

Sales clerks looked at me sidewise and explained things slo-w-ly and with Ex-tra En-un-ci-a-tion, so that I began to think they thought I was just plain ignorant! The soccer moms in the neighborhood asked me to repeat what I'd just told them for the amusement of the person next to them, and then the northerners tried to say a word or two with my accent. Sometimes I had to define a term for them.

Of course, this was going on in the other direction as well. I usually didn't copy their speech until I got home and tried it out on my own ears: "soccer" (sah-ka), "barrette" (bar-et), "doll" (dall), "Chi-keg-go," "want to go *with*?" "Da Cubs," "Da Bears." Then, new to Vermont, I listened with a kind of delight to the voices around me and their New England syllables, dropped r's, and expressions like "down cellah" referring to a house's basement, and where good things were "wicked" good.

I couldn't speak like a Vermonter or the way they did in Chicago, and I didn't really want to, but sometimes I didn't want to sound like me either. Being far away from familiar voices made my own stand out and at first that had the power to embarrass me. Later that very contrast made the once familiar, now missing voices seem more remarkable and particular. And the lovely thing was that I began to *hear* the stories in my head, hear a voice that was mine, and yet not, yammering away and I began to write as fast as I could trying to capture that elusive voice, whispering in words inaudible, giving me hope, not just for my writing life, but my daily work-a-day world existence.

I found other writers, some Southern, some not. My Southern friends and I bonded together and read every Southern-voiced piece of work we could get ahold of, talked about them, and soon began trying our hands at short stories. When I shared these stories with my new Midwestern friends, they admired them for their voice (so ordinary and normal to me) and made me feel that there was something unique to my voice and something worth doing with it. Strangely enough, in leaving the familiar voices and places of the South behind, I found my own tiny thread of it, separate, ordinary, and yet unique. And I learned to trust it.

Still, I had to learn something that surprised me no end: Even though my character's voice came to me as nearly audible, almost dictated, true to life, it had to be reconstructed for the page. The voice I heard *told* me the story, but I had to find a way to *show* the story, in a similar voice, but one particularly designed for my reading audience. This new audience was no longer only me. The ultimate listener was my reader.

Throughout this time of apprenticeship I worked to make my prose style and my characters' written voices clearer and better, and to "show rather than tell." These are lessons I continue to learn; my first drafts are riddled with these technical issues. But I have come to think of them not as regrettable mistakes. Instead, they open new revision opportunities for:

1. Passive Voice, especially overuse of being verbs.
2. Adverbs (ly) as verb-crutches.
3. Empty phrases like "it was," "there were," "suddenly," "finally,' "that," etc.

4. Sensory statements: 'I heard' 'felt' 'saw'—experience once removed.

   I learned that I would be true to my character's voice not by a verbatim flow through me to the reader, but by giving life to my character—heart, mind and body—a living active life. I had to learn to show through revision what the character "told" me.

For example, in my first book, *Old Thunder and Miss Raney*, a picture book for ages three to eight, I wanted the plot to twist and turn, and end up where it was going in the first place, but in an unexpected way. Raney and her old horse, Thunder, had wanted to win a county fair blue ribbon all their lives, but had always fallen short. That year, Raney decided, would be different. She soon was thwarted in her plans by a tornado, a quick and enterprising neighbor, and her own lack of skill. However, she still managed to attain her goal of winning a blue ribbon; in fact, she and her horse each won blue ribbons for different feats. The readers' expectations are fulfilled in a way that is first denied and the character's expectations are fulfilled through her very failure at what she set out to do in the beginning.

Part of the overall effect of the story is accomplished through a strict first person point of view and part through the use of idiomatic voice. Raney's voice is old-fashioned and quirky and her tone humorous. The voice is made up of a combination of diction (certain words and phrases) and syntax (the way the sentences are made and put together in paragraphs) that evokes a time and place in America that has almost disappeared, but that I had a little exposure to in my earliest years with my grandparents. Within diction, inside the words, are sounds that set the tone, indicate the state of mind of the character, and evoke emotional responses in readers. Within the syntax, the construction of phrases, sentences, etc., are rhythms that allow the sounds to make patterns, allow sentences and paragraphs themselves to have plot (a beginning, middle, end) so that they build to an effect and keep surprises coming along at the ends rather than earlier in the sentence or paragraph. The slang phrases, like "Oh fiddle-dee-dee," "What in tarnation," and "Indeedy," fall at points in Raney's speech that show her emotional responses while maintaining a conversational feel in the telling of the tale:

> *"Horsefeathers!" Burning biscuits!*
>
> *Well, I'd just have to stir up another batch, park myself in front of the oven, and take them out when they were just right.*
>
> *I opened my flour bin.... "Empty? Well, fiddle-dee-dee."*
>
> *Then I pinned on my town hat and scurried down to the barn to find Old Thunder. Puffy black clouds*

rose along the horizon. Looked like we were in for it now—a hailstorm, for sure.

"Oh, pshaw!" I said, and stopped short.

I hoped this technique would heighten the feeling of immediacy in the story allowing surprise for the reader and the character at about the same time. I also wanted to establish a voice that sounded as if she were relating the tale of her stormy biscuit baking adventure perhaps for the umpteenth time.

In my second book, a picture book biography, *Through the Tempests Dark and Wild: A Story of Mary Shelley, Creator of Frankenstein*, for ages eight to twelve, I wanted to approximate the English of the Romantic period without losing my reader's interest or understanding. I also had an agenda with the book: to show that Mary Wollstonecraft Godwin was a writer and a highly educated young woman before Percy Bysshe Shelley entered her life (a bit of feminist revisionist biography) and to interest the reader in going further and actually reading Mary Shelley's *Frankenstein*. In order to do all these things, I chose a somewhat formal and elevated tone and voice, kept research at the forefront and fictionalizing at a minimum, selected a slice of her life that might interest a middle-grade-aged reader as well as show that Mary was already poised to become an author prior to her romance with Shelley (indeed, her first book was published when she was nine). I also wanted a structure of story-within-story to echo the structure of *Frankenstein*, though in a much simpler and sequential rather than telescopic way. Because of this structure, I had to make sure that the voice of the piece varied appropriately. The narrator's voice had to be serious and honest; Mary's voice in telling the story of her birth and her mother's death had to be closer to what I might imagine (after reading selections from her later prose, poetry, letters, and diaries) that her own word choices and syntax might have been at age fourteen (with the consideration of my readers' ages and vocabularies taken into account); her poem-like dream had to look and sound dream-like; and her friend Isabel's retelling of a Scottish ghost story needed the flavor of a Scots' woman's diction in a story-teller's voice.

Isabel:

> *"On a moonlit summer night, when all the village lads and lasses gathered at the crossroads to dance and court and make merry, one sorrowful lass crept along behind and hid in the hedgerow. Her poor grieving heart couldn't join in the merriment and the dancing. On this night, a stranger rode in through the mist, leapt from his horse, and danced the evening gone...."*

While most readers won't stop to analyze either the different voices or the story-within-story structure of the book, this strategy for planning and executing the project posed fascinating challenges for me as I worked and kept me interested and moving forward. The idea of structure determining voice and vice versa was intriguing, inspiring, and, though at times difficult, ultimately gave me a great deal of pleasure and sense of accomplishment.

In the young adult novel, *The Painters of Lexieville*, which I first conceived of as an adult novel, I set out to write the story of a community. At the book's largest, it had nearly five hundred pages, seven voices, and, I hoped, cohesiveness while showing different views on the same events. The characters' voices, syntax, diction, sounds, and rhythms differed according to their backgrounds and personalities, but the overall effect was just too much. Juggling everyone's wants, needs, personalities, and points of view became unwieldy. This included the seven voiced characters: Pert, Jobe, Truly, Mrs. Turnbull, Katie, Lorelei, Brittany Lee, and later an eighth in the form of Raynell's diary pages.

What began as a story of a community quickly grew into an intergenerational saga about a state. It could have been two or three books! I drew and repeatedly revised a family tree going back prior to the Civil War. I even went as far as to imagine some of those people's stories, which was fun, but just a diversion from the real book at hand.

I had to manage the mess by deciding on a smaller and what I hoped would be a more effective slice of life: the story of a family told through the voices of the mother, sister, and brother. I condensed Mrs. Turnbull's chapters into social worker report forms and included them. Never in the whole process did I have the father's voice, even when I tried to hear it, so, in the end, he's just there being a loving, steady, but ultimately ineffective and passive presence in the family drama.

In early drafts, I simply wrote the voices as they came to me; in revision, I worked on shaping sentences for rhythm, pacing, emotional impact and words for sounds that fit the situation, the character's temperament, and emotional state. I tried to anticipate the readers' questions and answer them as needed with just enough tension to keep the story moving, but not enough frustration to stop the reader reading. I learned along the way that if I set forth the character's inner response patterns early on, I had to do less and less of that kind of showing as the book progressed, so that the events themselves would trigger in the reader the responses I planted. Here are samples of each of the three voices that remained after this revision in the final published book.

Jobe:

> *Time was, nothing had changed, not for our whole lives. Rain in the spring turned our road to a bog, and I fishtailed it for fun down the ruts when I was driving in the pickup listening to the top country countdown, singing out loud, never seeing nothing coming.*

Pert:

I opened the gym door and my ears filled with echoes, balls bouncing, rubber soles squeaking on the wood floor, and the bleachers clattering underfoot as the girls climbed up and sat down. But mostly the voices hit me, all high-pitched and giggly. And not one of them interested in whether I showed up or not. Except maybe Raynell, and she didn't count.

Truly:

I've held my forehead to this pane so long it's no longer a refreshment, no cooler than the spring evening air. Outside there's just pine trees, scrabbly stones, thin weeds, and pinecones scattered like lost children.

These examples are from the characters' first words in the first three chapters of the novel. I wanted to set up right away their attitudes, concerns, personalities, and opening emotional states. Here, in a prologue entitled "Before," Jobe is, with hard-won wisdom, harkening back to a more carefree time when he was cheerful, hopeful, and oblivious to what was to come. His sister Pert's entrance onto the story stage is attentive and angry, expecting nothing good to happen. Truly, their mother, is melancholy and lost. Because they are from the same family, region, and society, their voices would need to be similar, but their unique selves and individual situations influence their diction and syntax, giving them their own idiosyncratic voices.

In *Trash*, a long narrative-in-poems for young adults, I decided upon a more collaborative effort that would allow my readers to help make the meaning of each piece and of the book as a whole. It was scary. What if they didn't get it? What if this group of over a hundred poems became just a messy jumble of…trash?

I have become intrigued with more than one mode of poetry as I have studied it over the last few years and have come to enjoy experimenting with many of them, especially dispersive forms, abstract lyric, and formal play. I like the idea of form following content as well as how form can illustrate voice, indicating emotion and state of mind, and the wonderful quirky unexpectedness of allowing content to sometimes be determined by form. In *Trash* I wondered if what I loved about poetry, not just the overt statements, but its music, the effects of sound, line length, enjambment (the breaking of line), rhythm, stanza length, shape, diction, unorthodox syntax or sentence fragments, and metaphor could work to my advantage in telling a story—a long narrative, something akin to a novel in its continuous, cumulative effect. But I wanted every poem to have a different appearance from the one before and after it. I wanted the cumulative emotional effect to grow out of this difference (form following content), but worried that the difference might cause it to seem episodic. I hoped most of all that somehow these small bits would be conducive to a reader's moving forward in the book and not frustrate the reader. I hoped the bites of text would provide stopping places (something like chapters do) while also enticing the reader to go on for more.

Each section of the book is preceded by a header that establishes place, character and age. For example: *Vernal, Arkansas, Sissy Lexie, age 16.*

On the first page, the first poem, has no regular form, but progresses down the page jumping in from the left margin and using white space to provide emphasis and suggest time between words and phrases in order to give the flavor of Sissy's voice and to set up the situation and story problem:

Garbage

I hate
how

we breathe it
    wear it
        stain our hands with it
        smell of it....

The second poem is a villanelle, originally a free-form Italian, Spanish, or French country dance-song that evolved into an English poetic form with a prescribed rhythm, meter, repetition pattern, stanza length, and rhyme scheme. The music of the piece should come through and indicate something about the situation, the persona, or the emotion behind it. The form should follow the content, of course, but the content is also somewhat determined by the form. I found myself choosing a different word with a slightly different shade of meaning or feeling in order to fulfill the rhyme requirements. In doing this I discovered more about the character, more about the possibilities of the situation, and more about her possible responses to it, and, certainly, more about the influence of form on content.

In the same way a prose writer might indicate as early as possible the structural units, points of view, tonal changes, or other attributes of a particular novel, I needed to place a formal poem second or at most, third, because of the need to establish what kind of book this would be, and to set up the expectation that other formal poems might be coming later. I also wanted to show a kind of repetitive dance, boring and awful, the routine of life that the protagonist was struggling with, and with which the book would deal.

In order to this, I placed this poem next:

Each summer day is like the one before—
hot sun   blue sky   the truck   the trash   the stink
each night-time's harvest load of life's a bore.

Each minute's tick takes hours I can't ignore.
My eyes fill up & I try hard to blink
away this summer's tears. Like days before

I want to dream away the stench & gore.
I have to turn my brain off & not think
of night's gross harvest load, a lifeless bore....

Do you notice the iambic pentameter rhythm/meter pattern, a change in voice rhythm that signals a change in the character's emotional state?

What about the rhyme scheme? (*aba* in the three line stanzas, which changes to *abaa* in the final four line stanza, which is not included here.) A change of tone occurs as the character becomes less frustrated and abrupt (as in the first poem) and more introspective and down-hearted.

Do you notice the repetition? (The first line repeats as the last line of the second stanza; third line repeats as the last line of the third stanza/first repeats as last line of the fourth stanza; then both return in order as the last two lines of poem in the four-line stanza.) I like to vary the lines keeping key features to make them recognizable but not exact copies that parrot the lines down through the poem. I want the diction to seem natural, even in its intensity and obsessiveness.

In this book I wanted to show obsession through the repetitiveness, rigidity through couplets, dissolution through dispersive forms, and I wanted to construct my own forms, which were usually syllabic, five or ten syllables per line most of the time. I wanted the forms on the page to have a visual cumulative effect that allowed the emotional life of the character to be evident from the first glance at the page. I wanted someone thumbing through the book to have an idea of the process the character goes through without having to read the text at all. I wanted the form of the poem to be a visual representation as well as an aural one of the rising action, the unsuccessful trials, the obstacles, everything. I don't know if my readers consciously perceive these effects, but the idea of how form and content, emotion and structure might work, kept me going, kept me inspired over the long haul of writing and revising *Trash*.

All of us are inspired to use the tools we have to bring craft and art to bear in writing our stories and in so doing we construct our books, find our characters' voices, and eventually our own voices. But how? As Carol Bly says in *Beyond the Writers Workshop: New Ways to Write Creative Nonfiction*, our first drafts are inspiration drafts, middle drafts are spiritual deepening drafts (or what I call discovery drafts), and the final drafts are literary fixing. For me, these inspiration drafts are when I am becoming possessed of a voice and a tale. Middle drafts (second and following) are where more story is revealed by my going deeper, beyond the voice's chatter, by probing character, making character resist, and finding the hidden places character may not know yet (or ever know) within herself. For me, the mission of these middle drafts is to discover the real story and embody in words the spirit of the voice. Final drafts may be the fixer-upper drafts, but don't close down too soon. Keep the story going; keep it open to discovery as long as possible.

Each of our manuscripts is in one of these stages. Each stage is a process of hope and waiting. It takes patience and time to get the character to give up her deepest-held secrets. Her ostensible problem may be a smokescreen for the deeper one. The key is not to let the character off the hook too soon. In other words, don't let *yourself* off the hook too soon. Revision is where you discover the story, where the character's voice grows strong and particular. In not letting the character off the hook, you, as writer-in-charge, insist on keeping the process going in order to mine it for all its riches.

An example from life: A woman (perhaps from the South, and, okay, it's possible I could be talking about myself) may appear open, talk a lot, tell "all," but is sure to keep that one deep dark family secret or personal failing, fear, or secret sin buried. Her apparent openness tends to obscure her true lack of openness. Characters will do this, too. You may have to wait them out, pushing a bit now and then, encouraging them through this three-fold process, and moving back and forth from draft mode to revision mode as you keep the imagination open and as you hone in on the "truth" of your fiction.

Above, I said that each stage of writing a manuscript is a process of waiting and hope. So what's all this got to do with hope? We have to rely upon hope and have faith in our work to ever get the story finished (or started for that matter). We have to trust the process from drafting, to revising, to the fixing-up stages because it does work. It takes time and patience, but the process works.

But what about the "message" of hope in our work for our readers? I'm not one who insists that novels for young people must wrench some overt hopeful outcome out of the jaws of reality, but I am a believer that, just as surely as reality holds its horror, it also hands out hope. What can offer readers more hope for their own lives and their own voices than the kind of persistent inquiry into the nature of being human in a far from perfect world that writers engage in when we crawl into the skin of our character, feel his beating heart as our own and be willing to suffer—or rejoice—with him as he welcomes, resists, and finally embraces his own humanness, with all that means—the 'good' and the 'bad' together—becoming a voice through the word in the world?

I believe we hear the story first in the character's voice with all his defenses in play. We take that as a precious gift knowing that in order to find our own unique writerly voices, we must take his apart and put it back together, not as a *told tale*, but a *life lived*. Our job is to conjure out of words on the page and the workings of our imaginations, the worlds of our characters' lives. As convincingly true and real as our own. That is hope! Hope for every character who calls to us; hope for every story we bring to life for our readers; and hope for each writer who engages and trusts this process. Not only do we write stories, we write selves—ourselves—revising and renewing our own vision and our own way of being in the world. Revision is re-vision; re-seeing, re-living wholeheartedly with patience and faith, and sometimes fear—but always with the possibility of being one of the angels whispering hope.

Exercise:

Voice Lessons

1. What are some memories from your life: songs, sayings, idioms?

2. Take an aural memory and recreate it as scene, using fiction techniques (dialogue, gesture, thought, emotion, sensation, description).

3. Consider what significance this memory holds for you. Now, revise with this in mind, adding comments on the meaning you saw in it then and see in it now (subtle or overt).

4. Take it one step further by asking yourself why you chose that particular memory today—what new meanings have you discovered by writing about it—or if none discovered, take some time to see what occurs to you.

CHAPTER THREE

PORTALS AND NEGATIVE SPACE

I. PORTALS

At Halloween, that time of year when tradition and legend tell of a slippage between the world of flesh and the world of spirit, I think about portals: those doors, passageways, openings between one sort of place and another. In magical fantasy, we find keys to the passages, clocks that strike thirteen in the night, and a womblike wardrobe that leads to an old-fashioned streetlamp in a strange and chilly world. In horror, we find zombies and ghouls walking the streets of our world. In paranormal romance, we might find boyfriends who are vampires or guardian angels who want to be boyfriends. In time travel or science fiction, one era bleeds into another, one faraway galaxy wormholes into another, maybe our own.

Portals, scientists have found, cause us (here on earth) to reset our brains and prepare for the new environment. That's why we walk through a door from the living room to the kitchen to get a pair of scissors to snip off a wayward thread on a throw pillow and stand there asking ourselves what we were going after and have to return to the living room to jog our memories. Once we see the thread again, we hold that image in our minds as we recross the threshold and reenter the kitchen, thus making the thought move through the portal with us. This happens to us all, whether aging or school aged; it's a phenomenon of human existence.

I wonder if that is why the idea of magical portals originated and why the idea of passing from one world to another is so powerful in story. Of course, the original portal is birth into life, and the final one, death out of earthly life. What more powerful, magical, frightening, and completely normal passages are there?

On a trip to New Mexico my husband and I sat with my cousin in her adobe house's *portal* (a long, covered patio that wrapped around the back and side of the house) where we enjoyed a cool morning's breakfast and regaled each other with stories and memories from our lives. Something about that sense of being neither outside nor inside seemed to be conducive to storytelling, just as it had been on our old Southern porches with porch swings and wicker rockers. Neither outside nor in, we slipped between the old days and nowadays, and time lingered with us.

What can we make of this for the writer? For me, walking from one part of my house to the new addition where I do my creative work, reminds me who I am and what I'm doing here, resets my day's trajectory and opens up the magic mind for story. I have one place I sit to work on my student's writing packets and another, a window-seat, where I sit to imagine into the worlds of my own stories. Just having the outside there, so close at hand, with me half-way between the inside and the outdoors, sets my mind free to wander about in that realm between the real and the imagined, the ordinary and the magical. I can travel to the nearest earth-like planet with its orbiting laboratories or skip along a sidewalk with a little girl who lives on a houseboat on the Seine or travel back to Mississippi at the beginning of the Civil Rights era. I can be as silly as a cartoon-like prospector who loses his voice or a young woman in the early 1900's who gets sent aloft by a tornado. I can become a runaway teen writing graffiti or a boy plagued with thoughts of suicide, or imagine what it might be like to have created Frankenstein's monster.

When I visit schools and read the ghost story from *Through the Tempests Dark and Wild: A Story of Mary Shelley, Creator of Frankenstein*, I find the portal to the children's imaginations is our popular culture's depiction of her monster, green stitched-up forehead, bolts holding head to neck, and large lumbering frame. Through that initial image, I introduce them to the young woman who at only eighteen wrote a novel that came out of her own sorrows, the death of her mother, rejection by her father, and the death of her own firstborn child. Science was opening a portal to the understanding of electricity and of anatomy and physiology. The French Revolution had loosed ideas of freedom and equality, the new century had begun, and nothing would ever be the same.

A portal is a place of transformation, a place between here and there where magic might enter. As writers, every night we go through the portal of sleep and wake on the other side into a new day where in our stories' other worlds exist with our own, simultaneously real and imagined. Like a perennial All Hallow's Eve, our writers' minds allow flesh and spirit to work together as one to make story. For writers that is what life is about, making the unreal real, the real magical, and bringing the outside and the inside together, just touching, where our minds meet those of our readers' in the *portal*.

II. NEGATIVE CAPABILITY AND NEGATIVE SPACE

Can't see the forest for the trees? I remember laughing at that saying as a child because, of course, a forest WAS the trees, right? Or maybe not. We all have heard that the whole is made up of the sum of its parts, that it's all the trees taken together that make the forest, or, in the case of a story, all the scenes with their dialogue, description, and action that make up the whole. Some writers see the concept of the whole first and work toward finding the parts to make up the sum; others are masters of minutiae and start with the smallest components and work to find the whole.

Most of my stories have begun in voice and in place, a lone voice, disembodied, speaking into a landscape. Eventually, this voice finds its body and the place develops details and the rest grows from there. While I write, I feel like a wanderer in a vast forest whose only touchstones are the trees and rocks and insects and ferns. I move from one to another, searching ahead as far as my eyes can see through the shadows and hoping for the occasional glimpse of blue sky above or the guiding presence of the pole star for direction. I remember asking a friend in Chicago where her stories began. She said that the first thing she sees is the structure. I was dumbfounded. Structure, for me, came later as a kind of pattern into which I struggled to fit the pieces of story. I thought of my own writing as a crazy quilt, the pattern emerging out of the juxtaposition of the colors, the connections between the figures in the design, and the direction of the weave. I didn't remember ever starting with a distinct pattern in mind and making the pieces fit. Mostly, I just felt lucky that there was a subconscious action at work and eventually the pattern would emerge, as if it had been there all along. As far as my writing life goes, I've had to become capable of living in that uncertainty, of living in Keatsian *negative capability*.

Nowadays, I find myself absorbed in another aspect of the trees and the forest: the negative space between things. I know now a forest isn't as simple as the sum of its trees or ferns or lichen or stones or fungi. It's all these in relationship, existing in space and making open patterns between them.

When I studied art in college, I learned to see the world around me through its negative spaces, but that concept has been slow to enter my writing mind. When I paint or draw, I try not to allow my preconceptions of what certain objects look like to interfere with how they appear to my vision at the angle and light in which I am currently observing them, and instead try to draw how they occupy the space around them. In other words, I don't draw the antique clock on the wall, but the shape of the wall around it. From those lines and shadows in the background, the clock as it truly appears emerges. My vantage point, the light in the room, and my emotional state at the time all affect the way the clock might appear from one day to the next. If my point of view is directly in front of it, I see a very different clock from the clock I see at an oblique angle. But maybe more importantly, the background changes in the light and with the different distances and angles from which I observe it. The space around the object changes with the changing conditions and with my own movement and state of mind.

What does that have to do with the forest? Well, here in Vermont, trees surround my home. We live in a forest. I'm getting to know individual trees as separate from their other plant kin. I also see them in relationship as a part of a larger forest, but I am most acutely aware of the space between things, the way the branches bend and angle away from the trunk toward the light shining through the empty space, and how that space helps determine their rate and direction of growth. I notice the changing patterns of light and shadow on the forest floor and across the breeze-stirred leaves and needles. I glimpse the sky, blue-bright or white with clouds or twilight gray, through the grid of branches; birds move through the spaces, alight and disappear into them. Farther away through the negative spaces, the background peeks and unseen forces appear and move.

One clear blue-sky winter morning, I sat at my breakfast table staring down toward the brook through black tree trunks, noticing the white snowy patches beyond, their shapes and sizes, the light and color of the white subtly changing as the sun rose higher. And something moved out there. Far across the brook three bulky shapes moved through the white space I was observing. Larger and even darker than the tree trunks, indistinct, but definitely there. I believed they were moose, but I couldn't know for sure. As soon as they passed through the negative space, they were again swallowed up by the darkness of trees and forest. The scene appeared as before, except that *I* had changed and now the forest took on a life and a story it hadn't had before for me.

There, in that movement, was the story. Where the birds fly, the clouds move, the leaf falls, and the moose, like a shadow, passes, there is the true story of the forest. It's the minutiae as well as the large elements that make up a story, but they have to be in relationship in space, and in those interstices is where something happens. The space could be as large as the sky overhead in a forest glen or as small as the glimmer of sunshine on a leaf in the background seen through the spindly legs of an ant scurrying along the edge of a small piece of splintered bark, but it's the glimpse into that negative space that makes all the pieces become whole. It's the mystery and the unspoken, the shown rather than told that dwells there, metaphor and implication, dwelling in uncertainty, sometimes fleetingly, like the wind-strewn patterns of light and shadow on the forest floor.

Negative space isn't empty space, although at its most basic, as the white space in a poem or between paragraphs, it may appear to be empty when it is actually time and eye movement that exists there. Only in the space between can we hear the music of a poem or the voice of a story. It isn't a vacuum where sound waves cannot transfer. This negative space is filled with potential. It is where the story lives in all its uncertainty and possibility. In all its negative capability.

III. WHERE STORY LIVES

In the in-between space where the imagination sparks, where magical portals open and a new thought arises, where once nothing existed there enters a character, a voice speaking into a place, surrounded by other new voices, objects, animals, conflicts, problems, rising tension, joys and sorrows, failures and triumphs, climatic moments, complication and resolution, death and life: story. Writers go through the portal and into the negative spaces in search of story, the connective tissue of story, the 'what if?' that asks and answers the 'why?' in our stories and in our lives. Story, for the storyteller and for the audience, is essential for deep human communication. For as long as we have known ourselves to be human, those spaces between, between self and others, have been bridged with language of one kind or another. Through its connective power, story, gives us meaning and possibility.

Exercise:

Negative Capability

In 1817, Keats wrote in a letter to his brothers in America:

...(S)everal things dove-tailed in my mind, and at once it struck me what quality went to form a Man of Achievement,...I mean Negative Capability, that is, when a man is capable of being in uncertainties, mysteries, doubts, without any irritable reaching after fact and reason....

1. What does it mean to you to be capable of dwelling in uncertainties, mysteries, and doubts?

2. Write about how you might apply this idea to your stories, your life, and the act of writing?

3. How would the ability to be uncertain affect the writing process during early drafts? What about in revision?

PART II

THE CRAFT AND THE ART

CHAPTER FOUR

CHARACTERIZATION: CHOOSING POINT OF VIEW

Deciding on point of view is a central choice the writer makes when beginning to imagine a story, perhaps the most important one, the choice around which all other decisions pivot. But it's not as simple as asking, "Hmm, do I feel like writing a lot of 'I', 'you', or 'he/she/they'?" This is a central decision that has to be paid attention to and reassessed all the way through to the end of the revision process. Like it or not, point of view is the source of nearly everything else involved in the making of a story, things like voice and diction and syntax, perspective and distance (or from whose vantage point and at what remove that voice will come), tone and style, and even genre.

Some of our most basic questions about developing full scenes without over-writing, enlivening the story so that it doesn't feel flat, and deciding how much dialogue to include revolve around the central issue of point of view. In a close or intimate point of view, the objective will be to keep the main character's emotional state of mind available at all times to the reader; that is what "show, don't tell" is all about. The writer will enter the consciousness of the character at such a level as to be able to experience what the character senses, thinks, and feels almost as the writer experiences his own sensations, thoughts, and emotions, and will strive to make these apparent to the reader as if by osmosis. The character's point of view will be the vehicle for the reader to identify and experience vicariously what the character experiences.

In order to create the opportunity for our readers to identify with our characters, writers must be *fully present* in our stories, yet *absent from the writing.* What do I mean by this? When we are writing for children we may allow the telling to take over and the child's voice to be lost in an assessing, watching, reporting narrator and sometimes we even slip into our own authorial voice, which can come across as overwritten.

This problem of slipping into the wrong voice is also one of point of view. If you have an omniscient adult voice narrating the tale, giving lengthy descriptions, and making comments from outside the perceptions of the child character, you run the risk of losing your story—and your reader. Instead, choosing a specific point of view character and working within that constraint allows child to speak to child, character to reader, without an adult consciousness intervening and running the show.

Of course, some writers deliberately choose a point of view and narrative distance that doesn't require the most intimate sampling of a character's state of mind. Stories have different purposes and publishers and readers alike have varying expectations of different kinds of books. What I've been doing with my teaching at the MFA level, however, is striving to enable writers to go deeper in insight and in language to find the emotional core of character and story through a close-in narrator's point of view in first person or limited third person. Once student writers gain that skill, one that I believe is basic to the understanding of point of view, it becomes possible for them to access the entire range of point of view whenever needed or wherever their future stories lead them.

If you discover your narrator voice has intruded when you intend a close third or first person point of view, telling us in a very adult way about, say, the sixth grade dance, in revision you'll know that you need to work on showing all information through your main character's perspective, along with her evaluations and observations. The details she notices are the ones the reader wants to know about because those are the details important to the character. Early in a book, the reader is trying to get a handle on the character and trying earnestly to identify with her. Readers want to know what the other characters look like—through the main character's eyes—not from an observing narrator's (or author's) viewpoint. We must allow the character's emotions and reactions to color everything that is brought out in the narrative.

How do we manage to maintain an authentic young person's voice in our stories when it may not seem to come naturally? After all, we are adults, we have adult voices, and we may even have mature ideas we hope to get across in our books. Well, we keep the process going, keep going back, re-visioning and re-seeing the scenes from the character's point of view, going deeper and deeper into the character's perceptions, sensations, and responses, all the while moving away from an outside perspective. In order to do this, we allow what we once might have called mistakes in point of view to guide us back inside the imagined story at the moments where we somehow broke from it and allowed an authorial voice to intrude. Often, those "mistakes" are a kind of shorthand, a quick way to get our ideas down on the page, and are simply what happens in a first draft. Don't worry too much about it. Revision is when you'll layer your work, discovering more about your story and character as you reenter your imagination. Your task in revision will be to look at a phrase or word that needs revision and refrain from jumping quickly into a mental search to find a better alternative. Sure, that may be a stage in the process, but don't allow it to stop there. Don't settle for the easy fix. Return to the scene in your imagination, notice all the things you couldn't have seen in the first go round, take in more and more details until you discover the most salient ones. This could take reentering the imagination at that point several times, but it will happen.

In first person point of view, the reader will be able to have access to the character's emotional responses, as well as thoughts and sensations, at every turn. It is as if the reader becomes the character, knows what the character knows, and sees, feels, experiences all that the character does, just as we can be aware of our own bodily selves. This is similar to what psychologists refer to as "directly observable behavior." While in science this idea usually pertains to objective observation of a separate object or entity, I'm applying it to the more subjective act of observing our own selves as humans. When I say that the character can only know what she directly observes, what do I mean? How is that for the first person, the "I" character? Exactly as it is to be ourselves. In order to replicate this in your characters, think about the tiny details, the little perceptions, the incremental revelations, the flitting in and out of snippets of memory, the building emotions and tensions you experience as an individual in any given moment.

Imagine yourself on a fantastic journey, one that has magically placed you inside another person's mind and body, so that you become a particular eight-year-old boy named Michael. You can't see what he isn't looking at; you can't hear what he cannot hear. You feel his tummy rumble when he's hungry and his bare feet burn when he walks on a sunbaked sidewalk. If you've decided on first person, you will use the pronoun "I" and will write from his voice, his heart, and mind.

Here's an example of first person narration from a scene in Susan Fletcher's *Shadow Spinner* that allows reader close identification with the character through the senses, thoughts, and emotions:

> *(Zaynab) scooted the basket—with me in it—over the side of the roof.*
>
> *Falling. My stomach lurched up into my throat. The winch screech: a shoal of startled pigeons, cooing and flapping, took flight. Then the rope caught with a jerk and dangled me an arm's length below the edge of the roof...*
>
> *...The rope twisted and squeaked, turning me to face the dark palace walls, the city, then the walls again. I wrapped my veil close around me. The first blush of daylight softened the eastern horizon, limning the faint outlines of domes and minarets...*
>
> *...A shout from above. A scream. The basket plunged toward the ground—my stomach leaped up again—then the basket jerked to a swaying halt. When I looked up, I saw a eunuch peering down over the edge of the roof.*
>
> *More shouting. The basket began to rise. I looked down at the street. I could jump from here—maybe—but I would have to do it now.*

However, if you choose to go for a limited third person point of view in your story about Michael, you will use the words "he" and "Michael" rather than the first person pronoun. In this point of view you will still allow the reader full access to Michael's perceptions, thoughts, and emotions. Being as close to this character's consciousness as you can be will foster greater reader identification with your character and will naturally serve to raise the level of tension as the story progresses.

An example of limited third person from *Stephen Fair* by Tim Wynn-Jones:

> *Before anyone could catch him he was out the door, down into the woods. Down into Mordor, where the Shadows lie.*
>
> *It was a mild evening, a full moon, but in the deep woods there were shadows, all right. He had to make his way by feel, by heart. The underbrush closed in around him, grabbing at his bare ankles, clawing at his bare arms. Mosquitoes helped themselves to him.*
>
> *He came, at last, to a clearing dominated by a massive oak tree, whose branches seemed to lunge out from every side like the tentacles of an octopus.*
>
> *At the foot of the oak it was especially dark. He paused there, leaning against the trunk, patting it as though it were a trusty animal.*

> *When he had his breath back, he climbed up steps nailed onto the living wood. There was a platform up there carpeted in leaf-patterned moonlight. There was no roof. No walls.*
>
> *His heart slowed down, his hands stopped shaking. Around him the forest creaked with night life: the peepers in the swamp, the nightjars and nightingales, the hooting of a mouse-hunting owl. A breeze made the oak leaves tremble. And Stephen trembled, too, his centurion's armor no match for the night.*

In speaking of "limited" third, I mean that the point of view is very close to first person in perception, thought, and perspective. There is a continuum of third person point of view and sometimes in third person, even in "limited" third, the writer will choose to elevate the diction or in some other way be more flexible with perspective and distance than what first person point of view will allow. In first person, you are confined, in a way—though not necessarily in a bad way—to a narrower range of interpretation by the character.

However, when writing from inside a character's close point of view (even in first person), you can still subtly show things he, himself, may not be aware of so that the reader gleans more than the character knows. One of the great pleasures of reading about characters is identifying closely with the perceptions of a character, but still being able to observe other things beyond the character's own mental and emotional scope. That is part of what provides a reader with a feeling of rising tension in the progress of a plot. And we must not forget that it is the reader who wants to be the one who observes, assesses, and interprets what goes on in the story. The reader wants to be an active participant in the story's unfolding, not just be told about it. She wants to "see" it for herself.

In order to achieve an immediate and intimate point of view, take what you know about your own emotions, sensations, and perspective, and extrapolate to your character. Sometimes we may be allowing vagueness of feeling because we know the character is not clear on her own emotion. That kind of moment is precisely the one in which the writer can work her magic. If it is unclear to you, the writer—that's where the work lies. You need to be one step ahead of the character and in that one step you'll be allowing the reader a great deal of pleasure. When you allow the reader into the deepest life of the character, especially when the character herself doesn't know how to interpret her feelings, you are writing magic.

Often, we humans experience emotions and take action before we understand our motivations. That doesn't stop other observers from getting clues about what is going on inside us. You are in charge here, and it is your task to let your character lead you to understand things about her that she herself may never even know the whole book long. You may know things about her when she is grown and when she is old, things she couldn't possibly yet know, and those things will not even fall inside the story boundaries at all, but they will illuminate your understanding of your character.

Point of view is pivotal in understanding what is meant by the old admonition: "Show, don't tell." If you think of it as showing *and* telling, that might be helpful. There are things we need to tell to move the story along. The real trick is in knowing which things must be shown rather than told. You will need to show what your character notices even if the character doesn't consciously know the significance of some of the details she perceives. These salient details, ones she connects with and notices most as well as those that are more subconscious and elusive, give the reader the insight needed to understand who the character is and to begin to empathize with her. Some of these details will be shown directly in descriptive language, others in more subtle ways, in metaphor and through the strategic use of rhythm, repetition, sound, and white space on the page.

In order to render a full and immediate point of view, you may also need to include some of the character's thoughts, the statements she makes to herself. In a close-in point of view, you can let them arrive in the narration in the same way they arrive in her head, as statements without the unnecessary tag "she thought." Everything in the narration is from her mind and a true reportage of that mind includes explicit self-statements every bit as much as the more elusive twinges of the subconscious, the emotions, and bodily sensations.

Another way to achieve the immediacy of inner dialogue is to delve deeper into the emotional milieu. The point of view character as narrator (third person limited) makes it possible to allow the reader access to the inner workings of the psyche, even those responses the character chooses to ignore or repress. Often, I find in working with student writers, at the moment it seems the reader will be treated to an insight into the character's deeper self, the writer moves directly to an articulated thought that assesses the emotion rather than feels it, a statement rather than an image. What a disappointment when the reader really wants to live the moment with the character, wants to be shown rather than told. A test for this in revision is to notice those words or phrases that do not evoke a response through a particular specific image, but instead state that the character 'feels', 'sees', 'looks', 'watches,' 'hears', etc. Rather than distancing the character from the reader by talking about what's happening, strengthen those sentences to make the action happen onstage and in the moment rather than reporting it after the fact.

When you want to "show rather than tell," first shut your eyes and watch the action unfold through your character's perspective and perceptions. Don't yet try to find the language for it. Notice details of setting, gesture, tone of voice, and facial expression. Still don't try to find the words. Just keep the scene going and allow yourself to go deeply into the point of view of the main character, seeing what she's seeing, hearing what she's hearing, *and* feeling the emotions she's feeling. Once you've experienced the sensations and emotions, go back and write the best words you can find to describe each. Try to reproduce the mental, physical, and emotional worlds of your character.

In revising the passage, identify phrases that comment on or report the action, and work on bringing the scene to life with more immediacy and intimacy of point of view. Take the time it takes to show the scene, give details, write more than you need, and don't worry yet about cutting or condensing. That can come later, once you discover exactly what is necessary and what isn't.

For instance, a silence or slackening off of action provides you with the opportunity to delve into the character, to set up the next scene, or to have the character mull over what has come before. Many times, this opportunity is not taken even when it is obvious that something important is going on in the character's mind. Sometimes a writer will even say that the character was not thinking or that she did something absentmindedly. Those are comments that come close to a shift in point of view unless the character is thinking about not thinking or about being absentminded. Instead, if she does something with attention divided, you can show what she's really thinking about. Again, in first person and limited-third points of view, taking the time it takes to show the inner workings of character is imperative.

Another example: In Marion Dane Bauer's novel about a wolf cub, *Runt,* she could have told us, "Runt didn't try to follow the hunters again but lay down under a tree and watched the world and envied all the hunters." Instead she showed us:

> *Runt didn't try to follow the hunters again, but he didn't move back into his familiar place at the bottom of the pack, either. He found a spot at the edge of the clearing beneath some fragrant balsam trees and often lay there, watching.*
>
> *He watched the dragonflies skimming the surface of the lake, then swooping skyward again, their wings clacking. They were hunters, too; their prey, the droning mosquitoes.*
>
> *And the redbelly snake gliding out from beneath a rotting log, and the bats crisscrossing the sky. All were hunters.*
>
> *Runt watched and envied. He knew Raven had said that small could be brave and fierce, but would he ever have a chance to prove himself?*

Taking the time needed to show details of setting and state of mind allow the reader vital insights into the characters at crucial moments in their stories. Showing instead of telling, describing instead of reporting, and rendering scene instead of giving a summary statement are all ways of achieving immediacy in your writing and allowing your reader into the emotional lives of the characters.

When you are writing from a character's point of view, all information must come through that character's perceptions and must make logical sense. When your character is hiding in a closet and quaking from terror about a tornado warning on the radio, she would likely not have a conscious thought that gives non-emotional information to the reader about her small town in Texas and about the general frequency of thunderstorms there. She may not even be aware of "small town" and even less, at the moment, of what state she's from or its usual weather patterns. Establishing a sense of place is much more involved with the character's perceptions than with facts about the place. The reality of a place and a time require details only that particular character would notice and from her particular state of mind at the time. Try to imagine what details of place would impinge upon her consciousness while in an agitated emotional state such as fright during a storm. Perhaps inside the closet she would notice a faint odor of mothballs and the rough texture of a wool coat sleeve brushing against her cheek, music playing from a child's toy she jostles on the floor, the difficulty of breathing in the close and warm space, or the sporadic flashes of lightning coming from the small crack under the closed door. From the myriad of possible details, the ones you choose will be those that allow the reader greatest access to a particular character in relation to the ongoing story and in the situation she is dealing with at the moment.

Some technical issues that work against intimacy of perspective and immediacy in scene involve language that keeps the reader on the surface of the story. For instance, something like: "She smiled sweetly," and "He looked deadly serious." It is as if some outside narrator stands center stage in a theater, peeks behind the closed curtain, watches the scene unfold, gets the gist of it, makes deductions about the actors' emotions and reactions, then turns around and comments on the hidden action, interpreting for the audience what is happening in the play. That lag time and the intervention of the narrator's descriptions, deductions, interpretations, and comments build a barrier between actors and audience that drains the life out of the scenes and becomes tedious. Of course, after we read evaluative comments like those above ("She smiled sweetly," and "He looked deadly serious"), we can construct a vague image of "sweet" or "deadly serious," but preferably an actual *image* will be given in words for the reader to see directly rather than as a report filtered through a distancing narrator (or writer).

Other phrases that deduce the main character's state of mind or interpret what the character sees instead of showing it are ones like: "Flinching at the sudden demand," "His breath was crushed out of him with an 'oof'," and "The boy's expression was now one of amusement." Yet others might involve a passive verb construction or an adverb ending in 'ly' with a weaker verb.

In many cases the places that are technically problematic are also those that allow the point of view to slip. Readers want to experience exactly what the character experiences, so that they can evaluate for themselves, as reader-adventurers along with the character, what the situation really is. Readers need to have the same information the character does even if they might come to different conclusions about it. In fact, that dissonance can build story tension.

By writing with immediacy and specificity rather than offering deductions and giving reports, the writer allows readers to enter into the experience of the character. Perhaps instead of writing of a secondary character, "Mary nodded thoughtfully," for example, you might show what her face looks like as she nods so the readers (along with the main character) will then be able to see for themselves and make a decision about what Mary's nod means. Also, a character in the midst of an exciting or scary moment will probably not comment to himself that someone's gesture was done "thoughtfully," but will have a more visceral response to such a sight and to other details, such as gestures or facial expressions accompanying the words. That visceral response is usually one of a physiological reaction to emotion, not something that can be labeled in the white heat of the moment. It simply has to be felt rather than named. Those are the places where metaphor works its magic. Sometimes metaphors leap to the writer's mind, but at other times they are slow to develop and difficult to make precise. Often only after the imagination is engaged over and over in revision in an effort to hone in on and experience the reaction of the character by the writer can the right metaphor 'leap' into place. A writer's attempts to replicate life as it is experienced may not be easy, but it is essential to making the character, place, and story come alive for the reader.

For example, say a writer uses a shorthand statement like "Ann was shocked when Don glowered at her." This kind of phrase pushes the perspective far away from the main character's perception of the event and threatens to fall into cliché and melodrama. Because the story is "seen" from Ann's view, her sense of shock would be too overwhelming as it was being felt for her to take time out to experience it, assess and analyze it, then report to the reader that the feeling response was indeed shock. She would also simply see Don's face, see the frown lines, puckered lips, and then react, rather than observe those details of the expression without sharing them with the reader, internalize that image, analyze it, define and name it: a glower.

Another reason to stay close to the original perception is to keep the story moving forward at the intended pace, rather than have it slow to a crawl while readers pause to undo the character's analytical work and ask: "Hmmm...let's see, what does a glower look like?" and then have to determine their own image of what a glower looks like as a facial expression. Slowing the pace by slowing the reader's response to the story and can threaten the entire fictive dream you've so carefully negotiated between the character and the reader. It lowers the literary quality of the writing, and damages the pact between writer and reader that, in your striving for excellence, you have determined to honor.

In dialogue it is also best to stick with the good old standby "said" as much as possible. Attempts to vary tag lines by substituting alternative "telling" words rather than using those moments as opportunities to establish and reinforce your point of view character's state of mind stop the flow of the fictive dream and appear to throw in an outside narrator's perception and interpretation of the moment. You can trust that "said" does the trick more efficiently and subtly than "commanded" or "replied" or anything else along those lines.

Many overused tag lines ("I chided," "said with mounting excitement," "looked imploringly at me," etc.) point to that more omniscient narrator who watches the action behind the curtain and then relates it to the audience rather than showing the character's state of mind from her own point of view. This disembodied voice of an unknown narrator chimes in just when the reader wants to connect with character and inserts distance between them. In a first draft we might slip into narrator shorthand and write, "Micah cringed" in an attempt to show a point of view character's (in this case, Micah) feelings. What happens here, though, is the writer has moved from inside Micah's head to a quick peek from outside (as if Micah could watch himself cringe). In fact, an alert, detail-oriented outside observer would have described Micah's movements, his gestures and expressions rather than coming to a conclusion (oh, that is a cringe) and then reporting it. However, you don't even want the outside observation at all. In third-person limited, you want to stay inside Micah, feeling what he's feeling, emotionally and physically. Even if he were about to observe himself cringing, how odd that instead of the emotion felt, he is so objective that he can label it a cringe. More likely he probably won't even have a thought about his response, but simply have responded as a result of the emotion he feels. The response is what you are going for. If, indeed, he is able to objectively label his response during the experience of it that says some other things about his character and about how he intellectualizes his own responses. Of course, something like that can make for very interesting characterization, but only if it is what you intend to be doing with your character and your story.

Find a way to keep the reader involved at every turn in the character's thoughts and emotions, and the tension will rise almost effortlessly. Some things you can do to move the process along are noticing technical moments that work against you and using them to deepen the point of view in character. Too many telling phrases like "there are," "it was," the overuse of "-ly" adverbs to shore up weak verbs, or the use of passive verbs ("to be" forms like "was walking"—other than active ones like "walked") need to be replaced with showing language. Strong, active, exact words and images indicate the experience of the character from inside her body and mind. That's what we are after and that's what our readers long for in story.

Allowing readers to see the scenes played out will give them access to the character's state of mind and point of view. Scenes need action, dialogue, and narration. Think about expanding summarized moments made up of narrator deduction into fully realized scenes. Let the characters speak to each other, let things get thought, and things get done in the scene. Allow for more description and detail. Let the reader see through the character's eyes what her environment and the people in it look like. So much about the character and her present emotional state is revealed by the telling details she notices, the clues she picks up from others, and the thoughts and sensations she experiences.

The first draft is a way to tell yourself the story. The succeeding revisions will be your increasingly successful efforts to show the story to the reader. That's why revision is such an important and necessary part of the process of discovering your real story. You don't always find it in first draft, but in revisiting the moments one after the other and finding more than you could possibly have seen at first glance, just like entering a room day after day and viewing it from many angles each succeeding day. You will gradually discover the most minute and elusive details. Then (and only then) will you absolutely know which details are the most important ones for the story. In the same way, you won't really know the whole story until the details have unfolded through revision and re-vision.

With my students I emphasize the idea of and encourage the choice of a single, focused and deep point of view because I am interested in exploring character, believe in going deeply into experience, and allowing the reader to vicariously live that life in story. I do this for myself as well. It isn't that it's the only right way. There is no only right way. It's because most of us need to learn how to do this very well before we can go exploring in point of view. In the end the only right way is the one that works. If your aim is to recreate a life as nearly as possible, allowing readers to identify with people very different from themselves, then you need to understand how to do it. Maybe as time passes you will have other aims, which will necessitate your finding new techniques. Perhaps you will decide on a foray into second person or an omniscient or commenting narrator. All along our learning pathways, we writers read and think and figure out how and why others do what they do, then try for certain effects in our characters ourselves. Sometimes it works, sometimes not. But no matter what, we learn a bit more, and our writing grows.

One great boon of writing for any age, but writing for young people especially is that as you progress through your story from a young person's point of view, you'll be able to connect to your deepest self by going deeply into your imagination and into the stories of your life. You won't be writing from the point of view of an adult in the life situation you are in now, but you'll allow the young person you once were to follow an imagined path to a wisdom she and you may not yet know is there inside waiting to be discovered. The truest way to be *fully present* in our stories is to be *absent in the writing*, for us to have stepped out of the spotlight as story-*tell*-ers and plunged deep as story-*show*-ers. We will have given our stories to our characters. If they come alive, if readers believe and hear their voices, voices that have never, in fact, existed before, we will have succeeded. We will have tasted the magic of creation.

Exercise:

Practice in Point of View

1. Using 1st person point of view, write about trying to escape from something, someone, someplace, a memory, or emotion.

2. Using 3rd person limited, write the same scene. Notice this is not as simple as substituting "he" for "I."

3. Choosing either 1st or 3rd person point of view, write a stream-of-consciousness scene about a time when your protagonist is alone doing nothing but being in her own environment, making use of all that you know about what goes through your own mind at such times.

4. Rewrite the following sentences in the point of view indicated:

She smiled sweetly. *(Talking about herself in 3rd person limited.)*

He looked deadly serious. *(About another character from 1st person.)*

Flinching at the sudden demand, she vacillated. *(About another character from 1st person.)*

My breath was crushed out of me with an "oof." *(About self in 1st.)*

The boy's expression was now one of amusement. *(About himself in 3rd limited.)*

Mary nodded thoughtfully. *(About another character from 1st.)*

Ann was shocked when Don glowered at her. *(Try one from Ann's point of view and one from Don's, both 3rd person limited.)*

I chided my friend. *(From the self in 1st.)*

I said it all with mounting excitement. *(From the self in 1st.)*

It looked imploringly at me. *(About another creature from 1st.)*

Micah cringed. *(Try one about another character from 1st & about the self in 3rd.)*

CHAPTER FIVE

EMOTION AND REVSION: THE "EMOTIONAL CORE"

When a reader opens a book she wants to be taken into another world and become connected to it and to the main character's needs, hopes, and dreams. She is looking for issues that loom large in the mind and heart of the protagonist. She formulates questions and will read on to find the answers. But the reader can feel this identification only through the emotions of the main character, which must be made available to her by the author.

Research has shown that in responding to each other by mirroring facial expressions humans can evoke in themselves empathy for the feelings of others. One of Time Magazine's 100 Most Influential People of 2009 was Paul Ekman whose work shows that, as Jill Bolte Taylor, a neuroanatomist says:

> *Information about the external world streams in through our senses and is then processed and integrated by our brains into thoughts, words or deeds. And accompanying those forms of communication are facial expressions and the physical responses we call body language.*

Ekman's research over several decades has found that human cultures share the same facial expressions, all originating in the same forty-three muscles in the face, and that we use certain combinations to express the same emotions no matter what diverse languages or gestures we also use. Not only can we discern the emotion felt from an observed facial expression, but by simply making our own faces conform to those expressions we can, in some cases, bring about the emotion in ourselves.

At every turn, from first sentence to last, the writer works to foster this empathy in the reader by making the state of mind of the character available at every turn. By 'state of mind' I mean the workings of the mind of a character, the perceptions, sensations, emotions, and thoughts, in a particular situation. This is a hard thing to do because we have actions, scenes, and plot lines in our minds to pursue, and we just want to get on with it. But giving the characters actions or even thoughts is not enough. We have to get to the emotional responses in a particular state of mind; we need to get to the "emotional core."

The first question of several I want to address is:

What is the Emotional Core and why do we want to go there?

What we are hoping for as writers is to bring readers as close as possible inside our characters, to enable them to experience that character's emotions and sensations as well as what the character thinks and sees. This emotional movement of the story is the dynamic force that causes readers to identify with the character, keep reading, and be moved by a character's situation, problems, and attempts to cope.

In early draft pages, the thing I notice most in my own work and in the work of my students is the need for greater access to the main character's state of mind. As is perhaps usual with early drafts, much of the narrative moves smoothly enough on the surface, but the reader may be held at arm's length from the deeper feelings and responses of the character. The plot may move along and the character may undertake actions, but the reader is left wondering how it feels to *be* the character during these incidents. What does it feel like to be there—the sounds, sights, smells? Is the air hot and damp? How about the ways the character's emotional state impacts her body? Any stomach queasiness, mouth dryness, sweaty palms? What is it like to feel the way this character does at that moment? How would this particular character express her experience—directly or metaphorically?

In revisions, too, I notice a continuing need to keep going further inside the character, to allow the reader greater access to her innermost responses. Because full insight into character is rarely available in early drafts, we have to keep going back inside our imaginations whenever we realize we have neglected some part of a scene for too long.

The emotional trajectory of the novel and the event trajectory must move in response to each other. A successful novel will be a continuously cumulative exercise in cause and effect both in action and in emotion with everything arising out of what has come before and influencing the next actions and emotions. As the events progress, what is at stake emotionally builds as well.

The character enters the stage in a certain mindset and mood with specific needs, desires, strengths, weaknesses, and motives. Things happen and the character responds by feeling, thinking, speaking, and acting. Tension rises. Why? Not only because something exciting or intriguing has transpired, but because something changes inside the character in response. Emotions heighten, moving toward a crisis point. Again, not just a climax of action, but also of emotion. If we have taken the steps to make sure that readers are privy to the character's emotional moves throughout, we will have them right where we want them.

What are some of the writer's psychological moves leading to technical ones? In other words, how do you get your story from your mind and heart to hand and page, from imagination to manuscript?

In novels, each subsequent chapter will bear the marks of the one before it, not just in chronology of event but of emotional trajectory and resonance. Just as in life, what happens causes us to react, to emote and carry the residue of those responses as feelings from one event and setting into the next moment, next day, the next event, the next place. We are repositories of emotion carried with us from home to work to school, wherever we go, each place and experience adding its own layer of felt event.

We must allow our characters to be real enough, true to life enough, to carry along emotional baggage, just as we do. When a character is allowed the time and space to react, the emotion will be on the page for the reader to detect and carry into the next chapter. If we don't allow the emotional stain to run from one chapter to the next, the chapters will feel episodic. That will result in a loss of tension and a lack of cumulative energy over the course of the book.

In order to maintain and build this energy, the writer must delve into the character's deepest motivation, the desires, needs, and drives residing in the character's heart, mind, and body. The main character enters her story in a certain state of mind and with a set of needs and wants, along with a particular situation that usually brings about an inciting set of circumstances, and a story problem whose accompanying obstacles intervene to thwart the accomplishment of her goals. As the first events unfold, she responds to them out of that beginning state of mind, and these events will in turn affect her new state of mind, which then produces the next cycle of action/reaction. As the character moves forward in time, her emotional responses will grow and change, the tension between event and emotion will increase and story will be born.

To bring this basic human behavior into your writing, think of a causal event and ponder its effect on the character, then the underlying motivation, both conscious and unconscious, that has brought about this response. You may do this by asking the questions "What happens?" "Why?" "What next?" "Why?" "Then what?" and "Why?" Don't leave out asking "Why?" Awareness of motivation and cause and effect is the key that opens the door to the deeper reaches of character. You might even try copying the facial expression you think your character would make in her situation and see what emotion you experience as you identify with your character through mirroring empathy.

We writers try to put into language what we as bodies experience prior to language or explicit thought, such as impression, sensation, and reflex response. In doing so we are attempting to make concrete the ineffable.

First, there occurs a stimulus to which the character responds. This response causes something else to happen (another plot development, action, or event), which brings about a follow-up response on the part of the character. She will think, act, or speak only after she has experienced a feeling in her body, both emotion and sensation. In order to achieve this we might combine interior and exterior movements or physical and emotional details, keeping our reader with the character every step of the way, through an almost replicated physical and psychological experience. Or we may go into figurative language and metaphor rather than a clinical description. Too many times, even when we are able to apprehend the emotion correctly, we stay with a simplistic or cliché way of writing it. In revision, as we go deeper, through many layers of perception and revised language, eventually, let us hope, we will go beyond writing only about thumping hearts, sweating palms, and gasping breaths, and find a resonant language that *evokes* the experience in the reader rather than simply makes statements about the inner experience the character is undergoing during the plot events.

To get at character motivation, the questions "What does my character's soul want?" or "What is this character's deepest desire or most basic need?" may be helpful to keep in the forefront of our minds as we move through our stories, especially in revision. The events that impact what a character wants will produce in her varying emotional responses depending on advances or setbacks and her unique perceptions of them. The character will probably have one pervasive need for which she is willing to step out and take risks against all odds in an attempt to overcome the obstacles in her path, and she will probably have a series of lesser needs and wants that will come up—and get satisfied or thwarted—as the plot moves forward toward final resolution.

Writers are always wrestling with the balance of showing and telling in a story. There has to be enough direct and indirect indication of state of mind for the reader to share the character's point of view. If we begin with a good deal of showing—giving thought and feeling through salient details noticed in the world outside the character and inside the world of her body and mind—then it becomes possible to taper off a bit once the character's state of mind is established and has been shown through each successive stage. The reader will have gotten to know the character and be able to predict responses with empathy.

As with all human and animal behavior, our fictional characters function in stimulus-response loops. As our basic psychology classes teach us: All organisms are subjected to outside stimuli, which cause inner and outer responses, which in turn stimulate reactions and responses in other organisms and the environment.

If we consider the order in which we humans perceive and respond to stimuli, we might find ourselves showing rather than telling more easily. Humans usually respond first with feeling—emotion *and* sensation (linked, of course—the emotions are felt in the body), and then we form a thought or action (or engage in dialogue). At times we act or speak before we think, but not before we emote. The deep-seated, knee-jerk response is that of emotion. That's why we caution against too much telling. Telling is a comment, a thought *after the fact*, after the initial emotional reaction is over.

Through showing we keep the character's inner responses available to the reader as they occur. A reader cares, of course, about the action; he wants to see what happens, but he really, really cares about the character's response to that action. In life, there's little lag time from stimulus to outer response, but lots and lots goes on inside between the two. Readers know this; therefore, showing rather than telling is part of keeping faith with the reader as we strive to replicate human experience through the life of our characters. All dialogue is part of this sequence of human behavior: we experience a sensation, feel an emotion, think a thought, then speak or act. Of course, life gets interesting when one of the last three is altered from the sequence. Perhaps, as I mentioned before, a character might feel, speak or act, then think—and the plot thickens. But in whatever sequence the character happens to be able to operate, we will still find these elements.

Dialogue is made up of all the interior and the exterior elements of organisms communicating within and among themselves. Consider reading something like this in a scene: "They didn't speak for a while." Maybe in real life we don't speak, but it's much harder to provide the reader with a full scene without dialogue. Usually, the writer is letting himself off the hook for the moment and will have to recommit in a later revision. Of course, if it is important for the character not to speak in a scene, then other things have to take over, things like inner dialogue or thought, gestures or expressions, emotion, observation of details or perception through metaphorical image.

Even while writing in first person point of view when we must keep faith with the reader and allow the reader into that mind and heart, there is still room for a bit of caginess, and that, of course, is where the fun is. You may ask, how does the writer allow her reader to keep pace at every turn with the first person protagonist, and at the same time simulate the mind of one who is under stress, and perhaps unconsciously suppressing information? As we know, thoughts do not always accurately reflect our feelings. Thoughts can become a barrier between the character and her deeper self as well as the character and the reader. If you are going after the effect of unconscious suppression, you will probably need to make that a major issue of the story. If the character's suppression of thought or emotion is paramount, then over the course of the book she'll need to find her emotions surfacing and will have to try to cope with them. To the extent that the character becomes conscious of her own processes, motivation and memories, the reader needs to be allowed access to them. Also, a character might disclose more than she realizes, just as people in life do, allowing the reader to know more than the character herself knows.

At times, we will be able to give the reader a peek into these deeper workings by indicating something about how the emotional response is perceived. Even if she doesn't want to acknowledge what the response means in her thoughts, she will have felt it and the reader will have some hint of what's really going on. That's a source of suspense and enjoyment in the reader. For the writer, part of the fun—and the challenge—is replicating this particular character's mind, suppression and all.

What are some obstacles to a writer's ability to go more deeply into character?

1. Unwillingness to keep the imagination going throughout revision by keeping oneself open to new events and to new insights into character.

For me, the willingness to go deeper means I must commit myself to doing many revisions to make sure I'm allowing myself, and, in turn, the reader entrance to the secret reaches of the character and that I am allowing the reader access to the character's heart of hearts as if the reader *were* that person. What do I find when I manage to do that? Those are the re-imaginings that finally take me to the deep story, which is the emotional passage the character negotiates during the time the plot is happening. Only when I find my way to that place can I then invite the reader to enter. In some scenes I'm there from the moment of conception, but most of the time I have to wait until the character insists I follow her there. At any rate, first writing and subsequent revisions are like peeling away at an onion, layer by layer. It's slow, sometimes painful work. Don't be surprised if there are tears.

2. Unwillingness to go through this process or expecting too much too soon, being unwilling to make mistakes, or being unwilling to experience the emotion when necessary along with the character.

Sometimes in the process of articulating inner states of being, I have reached what I have come to see as a median, a sort of resting place, in the crossing of this sometimes dangerous and busy thoroughfare I've set out to conquer. I've become aware of inner states to a degree I had not been showing before, and I may be writing with more empathy and insight, allowing the character to reveal herself to me, and trying to find language to articulate what I am discovering. Now, how to step forward again into the fray and leave the safety of the labeling of feeling and enter the world of allowing the reader a more direct experience of emotion? A part of the answer is in awareness of language itself. In being aware of naming an emotion, you'll become aware of the need to go under it and show the feeling. How? Well, I believe that often you have to go there yourself and feel it along with the character. That's why it can be a dangerous crossing. One hesitates to commit oneself to what might be painful and frightening, to something that could, in fact, bring up real issues in the writer's own experience that have to be relived or remembered, and, in some cases, even worked through at long last.

Willingness, however, is the key. You'll find that as you become more willing, you'll be more able to "go there" with the character. It will also become easier to find the right words to show the feelings from the inside. It may take some quiet hours of contemplation, you alone with your character, staring into whatever abyss she has fallen into in her (and your) story. It may take asking others what certain experiences feel like. It may take some research into psychological states. But probably it is all there within you, waiting to be revealed.

Why do you think this particular story chose you to write it anyway? Have faith that you have the capacity to tell it to yourself, to live it with the character, and then show it to the reader, all of which is the process of revision. Revision is the interplay of inspiration and discovery in an ascending spiral—or should I say a descending one—deeper into realization and, finally, articulation.

One reason we all resist delving into the intimate point of view in either first or third person is that it means we have to be willing to feel what the character feels. When a character is going through difficulty—and what character worth her salt isn't?—the feelings may be intense, unpleasant, and distressing. But that's just it. That's what we've signed on for as writers. If it's difficult, then start practicing. Going inside (both character and self) is the pathway. Now, I realize there are times in our lives when we may be less willing or even less capable of "going there" and for very good reasons. We may have to give ourselves a break now and then. But we can never let ourselves off the hook completely. Eventually this work must be done. When the character comes alive, not only for the writer, but for the reader as well, a hitherto unknown connection has been forged. As writers for young people, I think many of us are aware that we want to be saying (and are saying) to each person in our audience that he or she is not alone in life's difficulties. With every story, we are whispering to our reader, "Someone has felt something like what you feel. You are not alone."

That itch of discomfort is absolutely where the writer needs to engage the story deeper and with greater attention, but oh, how difficult it can be! However, that discomfort is another thing the process of time in revision addresses. We may need the passage of time more than anything else to come to grips with some of the issues and feelings brought forth by our own words. Along with those insights, and with the greater understanding of the human condition and of ourselves as human beings that time provides, we, through the process of writing, may discover that we, too, are not alone.

The great twentieth century Southern writer Eudora Welty, in her book of essays on writing and literature, *The Eye of the Story*, said: "*Why?* is asked and replied to at various depths; the fishes in the sea are bigger the deeper we go." Plunging into the depths of the sea may be scary, but if you are looking for the whoppers, then you'll be rewarded. I guess it depends on how afraid you are of the biggest fish.

The good thing—and the hard thing—about writing out of our deepest selves is that we probably need to do most of our research about the human experience inside our own psyches and, to our dismay, we may find that we re-experience our emotions in ways we don't expect and at inconvenient times. One consolation is that we grow stronger as human beings when we face these feelings with honesty and courage, which is another function of revision. We are allowing ourselves, even persuading ourselves, to *be* ourselves in all our glory, but also in all our sorrow.

Because of that, I can warn you of rocky roads ahead, not only in the process of whatever you are writing now, but in just about everything else you will write from now on. Even humor has its roots in pain. However, I can assure you that those are the roads to the places you want to go. They are also the most scenic. And you'll find that sometimes the road itself is what makes the trip well worth taking.

Consider the changing emotions and mental accommodations people go through after trauma or during grief. In grief people move through denial, bargaining, guilt, depression, anger, and into acceptance, not always in that order. That sort of psychological movement is plausible and authentic for some characters to go through.

By the way, you can imagine how these effects of trauma or grief might manifest themselves in a writer's avoidance behavior. No, we don't always want to "go there" emotionally, and yes, sometimes we feel or engage in these coping mechanisms. Have you ever had to struggle with any of these in relation to your own writing: denial, bargaining, guilt, depression, anger, acceptance? If you have experienced any or all of them, know you are perhaps wrestling with the darker oppositional forces of our own human natures.

The Spanish poet Federico Garcia Lorca called this force the *Duende* and said art's emotional/spiritual source is the struggle with the "daimon" within.

He said:

> *Angel and Muse approach from without; the Angel sheds light and the Muse gives form....But the Duende, on the other hand, must come to life in the nethermost recesses of the blood. ...The true struggle is with the Duende....*
>
> *With idea, with sound, or with gesture, the Duende chooses the brim of the well for his open struggle with the creator. Angel and Muse escape in the violin or in musical measure, but the Duende draws blood, and in the healing of the wound that never quite closes, all that is unprecedented and invented...has its origin.*

For Lorca, the *Duende* resides in the...

...Black sounds—behind which there abide, in tenderest intimacy, the volcanoes, the ants, the zephyrs, and the enormous night, straining its waist against the Milky Way.

We as people and as writers continually wrestle with the *Duende*. So do our characters. What a dark and scary experience our struggle to make art may be upon occasion, but what a magnificent one!

In revision, how do we engage the struggle with the *Duende* at the level of language in order to peel away the layers of ordinary expression and get to the essentials of image rather than statement? How can we create a character that has a pulse when all we have are our own experiences and imaginations—and language? How can we find the right words, rhythms, syntax, and shape, to make true the emotional life, in all its complexity (its body, mind, and spirit)?

I've concluded that it's not only a matter of skill in revision, but also of honesty. Sometimes, I've found, bringing honesty to bear in revision is harder than anything. Seeing one's own experience of the world with a clear eye is one thing—hard enough in itself—but seeing and then speaking the truth of it is quite another.

So, how can we speak the truth as we come to discover it?

Say you have an interesting, beleaguered character with a real, deep-seated problem, an interesting setting, lively peripheral characters with sub-plots, and a provocative situation. You've allowed your imagination full-rein. It's time to work on some technical moments, specific weaknesses in language that may serve as re-entry points to the imagination. When you identify weak words, confusing phrases, or gaps in the writing, those places will offer you the opportunity to "fix" the surface of the manuscript by compelling you to re-enter the imagined scene in order to discover more story. Return to that magical place inside your character where the two of you meet, where emotions are felt in the body and appear on the page as image and metaphor rather than explicit thought. You are going to be entering emotion at a deep level and finding ways of conveying the perceived experience to the page in words. Mere words, of all things! Sometimes what we are trying to do as writers defies logic. However, at your disposal, and what you are going to keep uppermost in your mind at every turn, is your sense of the way cause-and-effect and empathetic understanding works in human beings.

An inciting event or action has occurred to propel the emotion and the action of the main character, and to draw the reader into the story. In attending to the emotional core of the character and the emotional trajectory of the book, revise by re-entering the story scene by scene, going deeper into character and emotion each step of the way. Pull out all the stops. You may overwrite, but that's fine at this stage. Put your all into it, go for broke, show all there is to show, and then some. Later, you can take out what's unnecessary. I've come to see in my work and in my students' work that it takes writing sentence number 1 through 9 to get to number 10 and sometimes sentence number 10 is the one you have needed to find all along. If you had stopped at number 3, you wouldn't have gotten there. You might go back and cut 2,5,6, & 8 and have just exactly what you need. It's a funny thing, but it's almost like the ghosts of those deleted words and sentences remain as connecting ideas the reader absorbs between the lines without having to have it spelled out. Still, the writer had to write those words in order to get to the next ones, the ones that become key to the character's psyche and to the author's real story.

I find that in writing about emotional responses, I go through several stages, many of which I subsequently don't want in the manuscript. Maybe I'll start with a weak verb and adverb pair, go back to find a more specific way of saying what I want to say by:

1. Going back into my imagination, those pictures in my head, rather than searching my thesaurus mind for another word to simply substitute;

2. Seeing new images, and keeping the imagination in play;

3. Telling myself in direct statements what the character is feeling;

4. Realizing I need to show it;

5. Going inside the character's body and feeling the physiological response the emotion produces;

6. Then, finally, using words as images to transfer this feeling to the reader.

We need, as literary theorist Helene Cixous writing in *The Body and the Text* says, to write the body, let body speak to body:

> ...*One cannot say the truth. One can only transmit it from one body to another.*
>
> ...*Censor the body and you censor breath and speech at the same time. Write yourself: Your body must make itself heard. Then the huge resources of the unconscious will burst out.*
>
> ...*All authors and all readers have experienced being wounded by the coming of the text, being wounded by wonder because the joy that a text inflicts hurts. Why does it hurt? When it comes to us, first of all it tears the night and the lie in which we usually live; it hurts to see the truth, but it is of course a joy.*

When you hold your own feet to the fire and coax the feelings into being and into the light of day, despite the pain or the joy involved, you'll be "going there," into the emotional core of your character and of your story.

Allowing the reader to share in the character's thoughts and responses as the scenes unfold, allowing more of the character's emotional core to show through is difficult, and can't usually be expected to come to the fore with power on the first draft. In first drafts you find the characters, setting, events, and begin to watch the scenes unfold. In subsequent drafts, do not to settle for what you noticed first, but continue to discover the hidden moments in the folds and layers of your story. First draft can be like entering a room for the first time. You'll notice things selectively; some very vivid images will remain after you've left the room, and some things other people might notice will have escaped you entirely.

In the first bursts of inspiration, a writer is struggling to tell herself the story. In revision, she is striving to show the story to the reader. In order to do that, revision has to take on much more importance than surface editing. We think of early drafts as story inspiration and last drafts as clean-up editing, but the bulk of the work, those middle drafts, are made for discovery, for continued revelation. You don't want to shut down the imagination too soon.

In revision, return to the scene, reentering the room of your imagination. Over the course of time, as you enter again and again, you'll come to know the room in great detail, and to see what was at first hidden. You'll look in the drawers and cupboards. You'll check under the bed. You'll go in and out different doors each time, and you'll spy on the others who frequent the space. On these subsequent visits, you'll discover more about your surroundings and come to know the people better. In the same way, you'll discover more and more of your story and more of your character with each subsequent revision.

The trick is to keep yourself open to new discoveries, new movements of your imagination. During this process, you'll come to share deeply your character's responses and emotions so that it will become easier to reproduce them for your reader. At first you may have to indicate what she's going through by simply stating it. Soon your new insights will influence the words and metaphors you use, and *showing* will become easier and more natural. The transition between telling and showing partakes of elements of intuition, but will also become more conscious, the prose more carefully thought out and constructed. This process of going from statement to evocation of emotion is usually accomplished through the use of telling details, details that only your character will notice in her unique state of mind, or through image and metaphor, getting beyond words while still bound by them. As you go deeper, you'll show yourself all you need to know about the character and her hopes, fears, needs, and desires. You can trust that. Emotion will show you the way.

In first draft, I seem to be "inspired" to write lots of passive verbs wagging their tails of spongy *ly* adverbs, but as frustrating as this is for me, I've come to see them as little flags to indicate places where I've used a bit of technical shorthand and will have to go back and work deeper until I find what's really there. I always do find much more.

Take heart. Those instances of technical shorthand we use in early drafts aren't really mistakes. Instead, they are guides to revision. Those moments can be expanded into fully fleshed-out scenes, scenes that contain narration, dialogue, gesture, thought, and feeling (both sensation and emotion). Soon you will be able to identify your own unique bits of technical shorthand, and then be able to reenter the fictive dream through those moments in order to discover more about your character and your story. For instance, take a phrase like "I babbled nervously." At this moment in the story, the character might be upset and scared. She might say, "I hardly heard her" of another character before she begins to babble. These two phrases, "I babbled nervously" and "I hardly heard her," are telling statements. It is as if the character has stopped the action and begun to comment on her own reactions. These phrases seem altogether too self-aware for the situation she is experiencing. Perhaps if the writer simply showed the other character (as the main character sees him) even with a very simple detail, then the reader could react along with the character to eyes that were, for example, "clear and blue as a gas flame." That comparison is visual, concrete. That sort of detail, the very thing this particular character would notice in this particular state of mind, is what you need to strive for in revision. Let the reader see what the character sees, feel the sensations that she would notice when in this emotional place. Show that she is rushing forward on the outside, babbling, because of her turbulent inner state. Show her heightened vision while her hearing muffles the other character's voice. Let the reader feel the exact pitch of her nervousness. Give the thoughts (sketchy here because there really is little time for thought), and the sensations so that the readers feel them along with her, so that if asked what she is doing here, they could deduce that the character is "babbling nervously," could tell you in a summary way what you have shown through taking time to put flesh on your character's bones and blood in her veins.

When I'm looking to find just the right word—one with the right shape to fit the emotional moment for the character—that's where I'm sure to find more story. Sometimes I discover new scenes, and always gain a deeper knowledge of character and motivation. My words begin to carry a greater emotional weight, and provide a resonance that has eluded me before.

Remember Eudora Welty saying *the fish are bigger the deeper you go*? By going deeper, we can find all that is necessary for readers to identify with the characters. We do it little by little over the course of writing draft after draft, revision after revision, as we go back inside ourselves and our characters, and continue to discover more and more. You can have faith in it. The process works. And you are not alone in it.

Readers may find events and action (stimuli) interesting, but without corresponding changes (responses) inside a character with whom they've come to identify, the story becomes unable to deliver on its possibilities. Character and circumstance must converge and ignite each other, rage for a while like a fire out of control—though the author at last proves to be always in charge—a story fire, finally mastered.

Exercise:

Statement and Evocation

Many of the statements we make about emotion can seem like deductions made from a removed position, an observing narrator. Some characters may be that self-aware and objective some of the time and under some conditions, but what we usually want is a more realistically human and transparent character. Statements can serve as a step in the process of articulating with mere words the ineffable, but for going deeper, you'll probably have to sit with your character and her feelings one by one. Think: she's angry here, what does anger feel like to her? Feel anger with her and discover (or remember) what it feels like in your own body, notice how it affects respiration and other bodily processes, as well as thought processes, then use words to describe those discoveries.

1. Sit quietly—aware of thoughts, bodily sensations, emotional and physiological changes—and describe what you are experiencing.
2. Imagine what a character might say in response to the above feelings to someone else who might be on the scene. Write it in dialogue.
3. Think of a simile or metaphor for this feeling.

4. Now, do this as you remember a time when you felt anger—grief—joy—pain—relaxed—sexy.

5. Take the following statements and revise showing the inner state of mind of the character (don't forget the use of metaphor):

Momentarily at a loss, Jimbo recoiled.
I roared heartily.
He felt joy as Penelope rushed into his arms.
Petitioning His Highness for leniency was the most difficult thing she'd ever done.
My spirits lifted, then were dashed again at the news.
The brew tasted awful.

6. Choose a day to observe yourself. Go about your usual activities, stopping about every two hours to retrace your thoughts and emotions. Think about the images this reminiscence brings into your mind. Make a few cursory notes. Then at the end of the day (or the next morning--so that night time awakenings might figure in) write about two or three of those moments that stand out most.

In rereading your writing, notice how sometimes quite ordinary things take on significance through memory and after close observation. Think about how some moments take on an almost luminescent quality, and how others seem to be seen through a tunnel, dark and narrow.

Ask yourself, if you had not been taking notes and intending to write about events in your life, whether you have even paid enough attention to remember them when you turned to the writing. Consider how your mind makes connections and how odd things crop up in your mental experience like *deja vu* sequences or through memories of earlier days or of dreams.

7. Incorporate all these (events, sensations, emotions, dreams, memories) into a brief story scene, either as fiction or memoir.

CHAPTER SIX

TWO SIDES OF THE SAME COIN: THE CHARACTER'S EMOTIONAL JOURNEY AND THE PLOT

As we write and receive feedback on our writing, we may find that we struggle at the juncture where character and plot unite. Or don't unite when they should. So, what can we do to make the character's emotional trajectory move along hand-in-hand with the story's event trajectory? Why should we even want to? Are these two things essentially separate or perhaps just different sides of the same coin?

First, what do I mean by the character's emotional trajectory, emotional journey, or inner plot as opposed to the story's action and event plot or outer trajectory? The outer plot is the sequence of events in the story that impinge upon the character (the stimuli) and thus cause or contribute to the responses that bring forth the change inside the character that leads to action by the character. We read to find out whether and how characters are able to cope with the things that happen to them. We love exciting story plots, but find them wanting when little change occurs inside the characters as a result of having lived through them.

Have you ever had an editor, agent, teacher, friend, or critique partner ask you why your character is doing whatever he's doing in the plot, perhaps asking what the character's motivation is for a particular action? Has anyone ever said that some action is "out of character"?

Have you ever had anyone ask if the character was the kind of person such a plot might happen to? Or suggest the plot itself isn't proceeding logically? Or maybe not proceeding at all, that nothing happens?

Or what about the comment that your dialogue is filled with talking heads? That there are no visual details to ground the story in the real world? That the state of mind of the character isn't clear? Or the point of view is off?

What about the comment that the character is living in her head and not her body? Or that gestures seem wooden and rote? Facial expressions or emotions "told" rather than "shown"?

I talk to my students about these things all the time and my editors tell me these things as well. We all struggle with the weaving of all the elements of scene together to replicate reality through artifice.

Consider the essential elements of scene:

Dialogue, the words spoken, gives information, furthers plot, and illuminates character;

Narration or exposition sets the scene, gives information, deepens character, and summarizes;

Action moves plot, gives characters something to react to and something to do.

All of these elements are used in a complete scene to one degree or another. Writers weave dialogue, narration, and action together to "flesh out" or embody the scene with character.

Elements essential to dialogue:
Inner and outer dialogue, thoughts and words;
Tags, gestures, actions, expressions;
Feelings—sensation and emotion.

"Feelings" fall into two categories—the sensory and the emotive. A sensory feeling is one that comes through the physical body in one of the five senses—sight, smell, touch, taste, hearing. An emotive response is that of the inner psychological self, in a myriad of emotions, single or in combination. However, we need to remember the sensory aspects of emotion, the physiological reactions in the body that signal or follow an emotive response, and that while we tend to think of these as separate physical or psychological phenomena, they are intricately connected, woven together, outer responses to inner sensations.

In previous chapters I've talked about how to get feelings into the narrative and have suggested using technical moments in language as potential windows into revision. When we identify 'telling' language, such as passive verbs, adverbs, and empty, non-image words, we can go back into our imaginations in search of active, specific, visual, and even metaphorical language in order to provide access to the character for the reader. Now, I want to look at ways of getting to the heart of the character while he or she is moving through the plot by studying some passages taken from three published books by Louise Hawes, Chris Lynch, and Norma Fox Mazer. Let's think about structure and about how to construct passages of dialogue, action, and narration in ways that will allow the melding together of two essential elements, or rather two half-elements, into one whole and complete element, thus producing a satisfying story. That is, the essential connection of plot and character needed to bring to life a complete and believable fictional world populated by real characters that we come to care about, identify with, and live vicariously through as readers.

As a reminder of the holistic nature of story, think of the traditional plot graph of rising and falling action most of us were taught in literature classes, a zigzag line that shows tension that rises to a peak, falls and rises again to a higher peak, and finally reaching the third and highest point of the story, the climax. Once reached, the story ends with the relaxing of tension, and the denouement. This graph is plotted on a vertical and horizontal axis, the horizontal one being the timeline and the vertical being the emotional pitch inside the character. This isn't to say that story has to be written chronologically to achieve this inner rising pressure, but for the sake of simplicity, let's just call the horizontal line chronological time. At every point, the line is intersected by the emotional effects upon the character of the movement of event through time. The horizontal time line will be marked by events and actions (stimuli) that will impact the character's reactions, responses that come out of the effect of the event upon the existing state of mind of the character at a particular moment. As time progresses along the horizontal axis and events occur, the pressure inside the character will rise and produce increased tension, pushing the line that represents their intersection upward.

That's why we want to make the character's state of mind available to the reader both upon entering the active scene and leaving it, as well as during the scene when the emotions and reactions of the character will be in flux. What is most desired by the character, the character's goal, will be under pressure constantly with obstacle after obstacle being cast by the antagonistic force into her path, thus causing her to grow fearful, angry, or frustrated because what's at stake is growing more perilous. As a result, she will set out to mount counter efforts to quash the opposing force. She will likely try and fail more than once before achieving the final resolution, which makes for a satisfying plot trajectory, one worthy of the emotional trajectory that accompanies it. Thus, the resolution will come at a climax point that is earned and is not premature, and not before the stakes have risen enough or the character and story tension high enough. Such a resolution would be anticlimactic.

When I talk to my students about point of view and plot action and their relationship, I find myself musing about how we humans really work. Things happen to us and around us seemingly simultaneously: we receive stimuli (things and people act in our world), and we respond, observe, talk, think, move, and emote in a blindingly fast sequence. Not long ago, while I was speaking to a student on the phone about how to revise her long passages of back-story into ongoing action, we got very animated about the topic. It was an exciting conversation and we were both completely focused. Because it was so energizing and we'd been talking for about forty-five minutes while I'd been sitting in a chair with my laptop getting too warm on my lap, I stood up and set aside the computer and paced around the room. My legs stretched and that felt good. I reached one arm above my head, then changed hands with the phone and stretched the other. I went to the door to let the dog in, along with a fresh cool breath of air, and the beauty of the world rushed into me, the rain-washed day, autumn in Vermont, all green grass and red, orange, yellow trees, black and white cows on the hillside across the valley, and the way the astonishing light traced newly sprung maroon on the heart of a green-edged leaf just outside the window. A bright metallic blue pickup truck went by, one that I'd never seen before and I wondered about the occupants and why they'd driven down this dead end road. Something about it reminded me of my brother-in-law's work with his son to restore an old pickup they'd painted almost the same color, the thought of which then tugged at my heart because my dad would have loved to have been a part of that work, but he'd died five or six years before. My dog stood at the window and barked. I shushed him and felt a twinge of hunger that brought an image to mind of the cheese sandwich I planned to fix for my lunch. And you know what? My student and I were still in dialogue, still thrilled with what we were talking about, still completely focused on our topic of conversation. That's when I stopped and told her all that had been going on in and around me as we'd conversed. "That's what I'm talking about," I said, "the way the present and the past and the future melt into the same moment of real time," and she completely understood because in her world the same thing had been happening, life moving around her and being reacted to by her even as we spoke so intently together.

Now, I try to keep reminding myself in my writing and, especially, in my revisions that I (and my characters) *live in all time at once—past, present, and future*—even if our books may proceed chronologically. This is why the emotional journey of the character and the action of the plot are all of a piece, inseparable if what we are after is replicating life with authenticity in our stories.

We humans, live only partly in the here and now; the rest of our brains are going like crazy remembering, seeing and re-experiencing snippets of visual and visceral memory, while we are processing incoming data and dreaming little daydreams of the future—what we'll eat for dinner, how our children might look when they walk in the door after a particularly trying day (one, in fact, that we may have been imagining in sharp pictorial detail, and perhaps worrying about, while they were away), or what we'll do when we are decades older, what happens when our books come out, or that picture in the statewide press of our readings at the local bookstore. We live in the past, present, and future simultaneously and the events of our lives and our inner and outer reactions to them are intricately intertwined.

Below, as I mentioned earlier, we'll look at some passages of dialogue from scenes in three published books that illustrate the ways writers can weave the two trajectories of emotion and event together in the same territory of the story. First of all, I'm going to un-revise some wonderful writers' scenes in ways I myself might have first written them—before I'd tackled what I call the "SOM" or "state of mind" revision. With apologies to the three novelists whose books I'm using and thanks for allowing me to do this, I'll show you those un-fleshed out passages, and then show you what the published work looks like. In each example, while we are looking at it to begin with, try to think how you might revise or suggest revision, then when you see what they have done, notice some of the moves they made to weave in all the elements of scene and all the elements of dialogue, braiding together the inner and outer experiences of the character. Take particular notice of how metaphor, simile, and descriptive details woven in add richness and resonance to the following three selected passages.

Third person point of view:

She had found (the thief) knee-deep in the watercress and rampion, bending over her plants, tearing them up by the fistful.

"And what be your business in a poor woman's garden?" She'd come up behind him, surprising him.

He stood up. "Forgive me, good madam," he stammered. "I only meant...That is, I was just...If you would be so kind..."

She said the first thing she could think of to keep him scared: "There will be a price, you know."

The fellow looked behind him then and when he turned back his voice broke. "Please, my lady," he said. "I means only to put by for my family."

And this, the original version from Louise Hawes' *Black Pearls*, the first story, "Dame Nigran's Tower":

She had found (the thief) knee-deep in the watercress and rampion. <u>The bells were silent and all the town dark, and yet there he was,</u> *bending over her plants, tearing them up by the fistful.*

"And what be your business in a poor woman's garden?" She'd come up behind him, surprising <u>him quite as much, she noticed with satisfaction, as the sight of him had startled her.</u>

<u>When he stood up, the moonlight turned his hair to ink, made his face look white and sickly. He had spilled some of the greens and was stuffing the rest down his vest. He was a long, large-boned man, but Tabby had seldom seen anyone so frightened.</u> *"Forgive me, good madam," he stammered, stooping to retrieve the cap he had let fall. "I only meant...That is, I was just...If you would be so kind..."*

<u>Tabby liked the look of his face, blanched with fear, his eyes glassy currants. She was ashamed of the pride that shot through her, knowing she was the cause of his stammer and his clumsiness, of his high, pinched voice. Awkward with this uncommon upper hand,</u> *she said the first thing she could think of to keep him scared: "There will be a price, you know."*

The fellow looked behind him then, <u>as if he were considering running right through the stone wall he</u>

had just climbed. When he turned back his voice broke and tears shone in the corners of his currant eyes. "Please, my lady," he said. "I means only to put by for my family."

Here we see how dialogue and narration can be woven together, giving the exchange a perspective and point of view through which to experience it. Notice, too, how the metaphors of "turned his hair to ink" and "his eyes glassy currants" add motion to the scene and give it a filmic quality.

Second person point of view:

"Hello," Angela says. She is half-buried in a survey of the comparative unit prices of Green Giant and store-brand garden peas. She waves a can, then gets back to business.

"Hello," you say. You continue on.

Next aisle, breakfast cereals.

"Hello," you say.

"Hello," Angela says.

Next aisle, pastas, rices, sauces and whatnot.

You burble at her. "I just never figured, I guess, you to be doing the shopping-type stuff, y'know."

"And I never figured you, to be eating, y'know, food-type stuff." Angela laughs. "What is with all this creamed corn, All-Bran, prunes..."

"My grandparents. I shop, for them." You pull your cart back.

She gets the message. "Sorry," she says. "Didn't mean to go there. Just making conversation." She smiles. "See ya."

"See ya."

Now the full passage from Chris Lynch's *Freewill:*

"Hello," Angela says. She is half-buried in a survey of the comparative unit prices of Green Giant and store-brand garden peas. She waves a can, then gets back to business.

"Hello," you say, <u>a little startled</u>. You continue on.

Next aisle, breakfast cereals.

"Hello," you say<u>, as if you have not already said it.</u>

<u>*Angela is walking with her mother and a bulging cart. Mother looks much like daughter, and not all that much older either. Good skin. Not as tall and muscular. Softer. Walking into a dance, you might very well make a run for the mom.*</u>

"Hello," Angela says, <u>grinning like people do at nuts.</u>

Next aisle, pastas, rices, sauces and whatnot. <u>No mother. Angela.</u>

You burble at her. "I just never figured, I guess, you to be doing the shopping-type stuff, y'know."

"And I never figured you, to be eating, y'know, food-type stuff."

Angela laughs <u>first at her own joke, which gives you the green light to laugh too. She's peeking now, and poking at your cart while you look all over nervously, as if she is poking around your underwear rather than your produce.</u>

"What is with all this creamed corn, All-Bran, prunes..."

"My grandparents. I shop, for them." You pull your cart back <u>away from Angela slightly, protectively.</u>

She gets the message. "Sorry," she says. <u>Sounds insulted.</u> "Didn't mean to go there. Just making conversation."

<u>You edge your cart back toward hers, offering another peek. Clumsy. Bump.</u>

She smiles. <u>"Thanks, anyway, but I've had enough thrills for today.</u> See ya."

"See ya."

<u>And she is gone and you are standing, like a cardboard whatever parked in front of an unmanned display selling old-folks groceries.</u>

Notice the spare prose, the almost lack of affect the second person gives this passage and yet, through the use of details, similes, and specific words, we get the juxtaposed feelings of self-consciousness and sexuality in the passage, ending with the last image and the descriptor "unmanned." What a lot is added with just the right light touch.

First person point of view:

The muscles in my legs were cramping again. The last time my legs cramped, I had leapt up without a thought and stamped my feet. Maman had been furious. "What if someone was in the house, you stupid girl!" Maman had never spoken to me like that before. Marc said, "Maman, it was an accident. She didn't mean to-"

"No," Maman said. "No excuses. Everything each of us does now matters. Everything. Do you understand? Karin! Answer."

"Yes," I said. "I understand."

Maman nodded. "All right, then. It won't happen again."

I bit that place below my thumb where it was still a little fleshy. I breathed in, breathed out. I breathed and listened. For heavy footsteps and voices shouting, Come out, Jews, we know you're in there.

Now the actual passage from Goodnight, Maman by Norma Fox Mazer:

The muscles in my legs were cramping again. Marc claimed I could uncramp them if I concentrated properly. I concentrated. I ordered my legs to uncramp. It wasn't working.

The last time my legs cramped, I had leapt up without a thought and stamped my feet. Maman had been furious. "What if someone was in the house, you stupid girl!" Maman had never spoken to me like that before. Marc said, "Maman, it was an accident. She didn't mean to—

"No," Maman said. "No excuses. Everything each of us does now matters. Everything. Do you understand? Karin! Answer."

"Yes," I said. "I understand."

Maman nodded. "All right, then. It won't happen again." Her eyes had that swollen look, as if she'd been crying for hours.

I bit that place below my thumb where it was still a little fleshy. My skin tasted salty. When the war ended, I planned to eat everything I wanted to, salty and sweet, and no turnips or cabbage ever again. Madame Zetain was very fond of turnip soup and cabbage soup, and turnip and cabbage stew, and cabbage and turnip soup. Whatever it was, I ate it all—and whatever it was, it was never enough.

I breathed in, breathed out, deep slow breaths from my belly, the way Maman had taught me. I breathed and listened. Listened with ears, eyes,

> *skin. Listened for a door slamming. For heavy footsteps and voices shouting,* Come out, Jews, we know you're in there.

This passage, like the others above, has resonance, gives information, and furthers the plot and characterization even in the version I showed you first, but the additional details about food, milk, and fleshiness of her thumb adds a dimension that otherwise we wouldn't have had. Also, it's very possible that the author wanted to get this information across, but didn't want to stop the action and have a long passage of telling. Instead, the characters are in relationship, action and threat is resident downstairs, and we get background, memory, and current emotional state of mind all in less than two short pages of text.

I hope you will be inspired to try this yourself. Take some passages you admire from your favorite books and pay particular attention to what the author has done to make the character and the plot action work together as one, and then set out to do the same as you revise your stories.

Melding the character's emotional trajectory with the plot trajectory is essential if we want to replicate the human point of view whether in first, second, or third person. We need to look at large blocks of narrative and long sections of back and forth dialogue and see where we can braid together the inner and outer experiences, the dialogue and narration and action, to form a whole, to allow our readers to experience a particular character's responses to a particular set of events. A story cannot have a character without action or plot without character response. A story is a whole mass of interconnections, outer world colliding with inner, just as it is for us in life.

The craft of writing allows us to use our imaginations to create new worlds, new characters, new events and to weave them together with the skills we work to develop all our writing lives. This task is our challenge and our joy.

Exercise:

Exploring Emotion Over Time

1. Story Question

Fill in the blanks: Will _____ (*your main character*) be able to _____ (*desired goal*), despite _____ (*first obstacle*), despite ____ (*next obstacle*), despite ___ (*etc. until you get all your plot complications listed*) and, in so doing, discover _____ (*satisfying resolution*)?

What would the character's response be after each obstacle? (Be sure to include both action and emotional response.)

How do those responses lead to next action, which will, in turn, set up the next obstacle?

2. Major/Minor Dramatic Questions

What is the overall story question? (Major Dramatic Question—*MDQ*) What questions do the chapters ask and answer throughout the story? (minor dramatic questions—*mdq*)

How do these minor questions develop and finally answer the Major Dramatic Question?

On first notecard write the Major Dramatic Question.

Use one notecard per chapter, one minor dramatic question per chapter.

List events in the chapter.

Note progress toward goal (forward, backward, stalemate) and obstacles raised.

List characters in the chapter's scenes, noting state of mind at entry and exit of each scene and each chapter.

CHAPTER SEVEN

THE PLOT OF THE SENTENCE: SOME TACTICS OF SYNTAX

When I told my husband I was going to write about the plot of the sentence, he raised an eyebrow and frowned. I went on, "You know, a sentence has a beginning, middle, and an end, just like most traditional plots."

He laughed. "Oh, I thought you said the 'plod' of the sentence, like in the book I'm reading."

He was reading *The Golden Bowl* by Henry James, and just the day before had told me he'd never seen so many long sentences containing individual words set off by commas. He found out that the text had been dictated by Henry James and when we wondered how that might have affected the punctuation, we surmised that whenever James paused, the scribe had stuck in a comma or a semicolon and just kept that sentence going on and on and on.

No, I'm not going to examine the plod of the sentence, at least not in that sense, although we have all probably written our share of plodding sentences, either too long or too boring, too passive or awkwardly paced. What got me started thinking about this topic is that I've sometimes found myself writing "Where's the *ta-da!*" in response to student writing as a way of trying to express what was missing in some of the sentences in a manuscript. Each instance was in relation to a sentence that didn't quite live up to its needed and potential effect in the location it occurred, often at the beginning or end of an essay, story, or chapter. Let's think about those places in our sentences, pivotal moments where we might have engaged our readers emotionally as well as intellectually, but somehow failed to do so.

What is that spark that causes the sentence to build and, in effect, come to a crescendo at the perfect moment? It has to do with the writer's decisions, usually in revision, about how to orchestrate and fine tune the sentence. In the same way a composer invents a dramatic variation in a musical theme, writers can vary the elements that make up sentences (rhythms, sounds, the placement and choice of words and phrases, the time it takes to read—slowing or speeding up the pace, tone and voice) to evoke responses in our audience, either to sustain the fictive dream in our stories or to make our cases in essays. I'm not going to go into great detail about larger structural strategies here, but attempt to keep our focus mostly at the sentence level where incrementally we induce our readers to agree with our arguments or to be motivated to keep turning the pages of our stories.

The basic building blocks of story structure are the beginning, middle, and end. These work together to build in a cumulative and continuous way, one event causing a subsequent effect and the effect becoming or contributing to the new cause and the next effect: a chain reaction, one thing leading to another and then another until resolution is reached and at least a temporary stasis is established. Sentences, too, have beginnings, middles, and ends, and these elements can be used to create voice, tone, mood, suspense, emphasis, rhythm, tension and pacing, and other desired effects. One of our most useful tools in revision is the strategic placement in sentences of words and phrases whose contexts and sounds offer a pliable medium for meaning and for emphasis.

We don't vary sentence structure just to provide relief from the aural monotony of the subject-verb-predicate construction although that is an important consideration in revision. While we pay attention to sound and sense, we also employ the same kinds of strategies we use in making a critical argument or developing a story plot. Each sentence has its own story to tell.

While we may consider the order in which sentences fall in a paragraph, building the plot of the paragraph to fulfill the needs of its placement in the overall story or essay, we may think less often of the words in sentences in this way.

In essays, we try to set forth the thesis statement early enough in the body of the essay to allow the audience a clear view of what to expect from the overall case being made. In subsequent paragraphs we build the argument through reasoning, evidence, and example. Out of that grows the conclusion, the crescendo and cymbal crash of emphasis to the essay. The thesis statement is not only fulfilled, but it is also expanded upon, opened up to new possibilities.

The same goes for story strategies. A character is introduced who has a problem that destabilizes the world of that character, and through trial and error, obstacles, conflict, set-backs and recoveries, stasis is regained, and resolution is reached, either through failure to overcome or success in overcoming the problem. Each paragraph, strategically placed just as in an essay, makes up the structural argument of the story and this arrangement of the paragraphs and chapters determines the story's readability and plausibility.

How often, though, do we think about this kind of structural strategy, the tactics of syntax or the planned arrangement of words, when we want to produce a particular desired effect inside a sentence? Well, you might say that is what we do any time we write words down in any sensible order, and you'd be right. We build structures that make meaning right from the first drafts, but we don't know yet what pressures these early sentences will have to bear in order to deliver the desired tone, mood, voice, and discovered meaning of an essay's or story's argument by the time the last drafts are written. If we concede that revision is a process of continual discovery as we write, then we can see the need to make sure the whole text of the essay or story reflects this discovery process and prepares the reader for the eventual clinching of the argument or the satisfying resolution of the story.

The first step in the presentation of a story is the setup, and in that setup, the spotlight shines upon the first sentence. It signals what kind of story we can expect, it gives us the first sound of the voice of the story, and, for some readers, may determine whether they keep reading or put the book down and go make a cheese sandwich.

For example, here is a sentence from the beginning of a story:

Corinne was awakened by the sound of yelling the night she decided to run away.

This gives us instant interest, instant plot and character tension, but not a clear understanding of the cause and effect of the elements. Emphasis falls upon the last words, "run away." Does she decide to run away as a result of waking to yelling or had she already decided to run away and then was awakened by yelling unrelated to that decision? It's not clear. What might happen if we look at the three sentence elements separately and work on a strategy for different placement?

We have: 1) Corinne was awakened; 2) by the sound of yelling; 3) the night she decided to run away—beginning, middle, end.

An alternate might be:

The night Corinne decided to run away she woke to the sound of yelling.

This one sets out the character and the situation of the novel right at the beginning (character has made a decision to run away), gives her action (wakes) in response to the drama of the moment, emphasizing the word "yelling," but still doesn't give a cause and effect relationship between the decision and the yelling, if, indeed, there is one.

A second alternative:

Yelling woke Corinne the night she decided to run away.

This leads with high drama, an event acting upon the character, and then ends with what we might surmise to be the response, the upshot, and introduces a further tension producer.

A third variation:

Yelling woke Corinne the night she ran away.

Here we have a strong stimulus that provokes action, and that action sets the story in motion.

For another example, let's take the first two sentences from the beginning of a novel:

The hill just below our cabin is full of bluebonnets. Their blooms are so blue they almost look purple in the sunset after the rain.

What do these two first sentences signal about the story we are about to read? Maybe an historical time period in a place where a character lives who is in tune with nature? Maybe; maybe not. Here we see a potentially beautiful image that deserves a more elegant syntax, a planned arrangement of words that make a strong evocative picture, one that gives us not only setting, but tone and mood, a mood that helps us determine what kind of story this will be and whether we want to continue reading. In this example, the images enter our minds as information because they've been stated, but the images are generic rather than specific, general impressions of a hill, a cabin, bluebonnets, sunset, and rain. What could the writer do to make us see the vision she sees and maybe hear the voice she hears, too? She might think about the argument or plot of the sentences, as well as working on finding active verbs. She might think about the order in which the words appear and ponder whether this is the best order of importance for the story she is going to tell.

In the original we see first the hill, then 'our' cabin, bluebonnets, blooms, blue, purple, sunset, rain. She might try something like this:

Covering the hill below our cabin, bluebonnets like a deep purple-blue carpet bloom in the sunset after the rain.

Because 'covering the hill below our cabin' isn't the strongest image or construction and there is no strategic need to delay 'bluebonnets', she might try again:

Bluebonnets, like a deep purple-blue carpet rolled out across the hill below our cabin, bloom in the sunset after the rain.

The first image then becomes the bluebonnets, deep purple-blue, so thick they resemble a carpet over the hill below. The next is 'our' cabin, and then the detail of sunset after rain. However, while the writer may be pleased with the beginning of the sentence and even the more subtle tucking into its middle of the view or 'our' cabin, she might wonder if there is more to be done with the ending of the sentence. She might ask herself why she wants that image there in the first place? It's nice, but not particularly important, as it stands now, to the set up of the story or characterization, tone, mood, or voice. Trusting that her subconscious gave her this image for a reason, the writer might ponder other details that will allow the image to deliver more resonance and other arrangements that will allow the sentence ending to provide more connection to the next sentence and the next paragraph and so on into the whole book. Again, through the process of continual discovery, she might try some more rearranging:

Bluebonnets bloom in the rain-washed sunset, a deep purple-blue carpet rolled out across the hill below our cabin.

This arrangement allows an ending emphasis to fall upon 'our cabin', so we might expect the next sentence to go on to say something about the cabin or the people who live there with the narrator. Here, though, to my inner ear, the 'bl' sounds get too heavy (bluebonnets, bloom, blue, below) and detract from the image and lend a kind of blubbering and muddy sound to the whole thing. It is also hard to read aloud. At this point, the writer might be surprised to find all that alliteration and repetitiveness in her sentence and think about scrapping it and starting over, which might be a good idea. However, let's keep using what we have, changing elements here and there to suit the needs of the story. By the way, you will have noticed the changing punctuation in these examples, though I have not pointed it out directly. Setting off dependent clauses with commas and fragmenting the sentences with periods (or combining sentences) become important tools to signal meaning, pace, and even voice. Here are a few possibilities:

First, the writer could take advantage of the 'bl' sounds if that is true to the mood of the piece, changing a few words, adding some story bait, and maybe even breaking up the long sentences into two or using fragments for ease of reading and for rhythm and pacing and other elements of voice:

Bluebonnets bloom in the rain-washed dusk. Like a purple-blue bruise staining the hill below our cabin. Jamie and me, we wait without lighting the candles for news. News of my best friend Cynthia Ann Parker and the Comanches who took her.

Or, for another kind of story:

Bluebonnets, a deep purple-blue carpet, roll out across the hill below our cabin. They glow in the rain-washed evening light just like Mama's eyes after a good homesick-for-kinfolks cry.

And another:

Like a deep purple shroud over the hill below the cabin, bluebonnets try to bloom in the near dark after rain.

The way Aunt Maudie says I will once I forget all about Mammy, Pappy, baby Seth—and the flood.

Which syntactical strategy solution to choose? That depends upon the kind of story you are writing and on how you want the reader to enter the book, with what mood and what expectation. The first sentences may change many times while the drafts and revisions go on, of course, and we may not know the real beginning till the end has been reached, but it never hurts to start thinking early about strategies for sentence-making and what reactions you might want them to evoke in the reader and at what position in the book, the paragraph, the chapter.

When I'm reading an ending sentence, the last one in a chapter, story, or essay in my students' work or even published material, I sometimes feel an almost physical need for a few more rhythmic beats or a different pattern of beats at the end, something that has a cadence that slows then builds like a crescendo in music. Sometimes it is simply not enough to get the right information into a sentence for the reader; we need to get a satisfying experience across in the words, sounds, and pacing. After readers have invested time and energy in reading a work, they need an ending that confirms that their emotional investment has been well used—and well rewarded.

In addition to sentence construction and word placement for content, clarity, and dramatic build, we can employ similar strategies for rhythm, sound, and cadence.

Let's take a quick look again at the four *Corinne* sentences we worked with at the beginning of this chapter. Read them aloud and listen to the way the rhythm and number of syllables in the words speed or slow the pace of your reading.

If you listen to the rhythm, you can determine and mark the stressed and unstressed syllables and get a visual representation that partially explains why a sentence might seem awkward and unwieldy. Notice the stumbling pattern of several unstressed syllables in the original sentence:

_ / _ _/ _ _ _ / _ / _ _ /
Corinne was awak<u>ened</u> <u>by the</u> sound of yelling the night
_ _ / _ _ / _ /
she decided to run away.

The passive verb construction led to a less active rhythm in the sentence. It's not only a matter of excess words, but of the 'rhythm static' excess words cause. Here it slows the sentence and makes for rhythms and sounds that fight the sense or meaning of the words themselves. Where the moment should be fraught with tension and foreboding (not to mention be the kick-off of the entire story), it stumbles slowly across the floor. If the writer had wanted to show a person half asleep, not alarmed, and perhaps bumbling her way down the hall to the bathroom at midnight, this rhythm could possibly work. But not here, not for this situation, and not for this story.

For a less awkward rhythm we might change this to:

_ / _ / _ _ / _ / _ _ / _ _
Corinne awoke to the sound of yelling the night she de-
/ _ _ / _ /
cided to run away.

At the very least this new rhythm is easier to read aloud and smoother on the inner ear when read silently.

Now, let's go back and examine our first rearrangement of sentence elements:

_ / _ / _ / _ _ / _ / _ / _ _
1) *The night Corinne decid<u>ed</u> <u>to run</u> away she woke <u>to the</u>*
/ _ / _
<u>*sound*</u> *of yelling.*

This sentence is made up of the most natural English meter, iambic (da-DUM, da-DUM, da-DUM), interspersed with its close variation, the anapest (da-da-DUM). Even though this gives us a kind of galloping beat, which, considering the sense of running away, could work, in this particular dramatic situation, the sentence still feels too full of beats, which may be caused by the galloping rhythm also being applied to the phrase 'to the sound'.

That might have worked better if the sound were drumming instead of yelling. So...the writer may try to simpli-simplify it to a more regular iambic rhythm:

    _   /   _   /   _ / _ /   _   / _ / _
1a) *The night Corinne decided she would run away she*
/   _ / _
woke to yelling.

This revision moves the sentence faster over the tongue and through the brain and gets the reader on into the next sentence and next action with ease even though the last syllable isn't stressed and weakens the feel of the action.

Our second recombination of elements:

  / _   /   _   /   _   /   _ _ /_ _ /
2) *Yelling woke Corinne the <u>night she decided to</u> run*
_ /
away.

In sentence number two, the rhythm begins in trochaic and shifts the anapestic to dactylic, both with their more forceful stresses on the initial beat of the metric feet. The effect of this beat on the first syllable "yell" almost makes the reader hear a yell and the DA-dum-dum switch from the da-da-DUM provides as much galloping speed as in sentence number one, but is more pressurized, being, as it is, less like our normal, natural English pattern of speech. Leaving the sentence on a stressed beat, too, lends energy to the action in the sentence and propels the reader forward to the next sentence and the next action.

Now, let's look back at our third combination, the one that was most effective for meaning and determine if we can tell from its rhythm another reason it succeeded where others might not have worked so well:

/ _ / _ / _ / _ / _ /
3) *Yelling woke Corinne the night she ran away.*

This sentence with its trochees and their initial stressed and trailing unstressed syllables, is strong and active and moves the reader swiftly and efficiently into the next moment, ending as it does on the first stressed beat of a trochaic foot. No chance the writer is going to lose the reader between first and second sentences.

Feel the speed of this line as you read it aloud:

Yelling woke Corinne the night she ran away.

Even if you aren't a poet who rattles off words like iamb, trochee, anapest, dactyl, spondee and such, don't worry. (I'm not really one of those either.) There's no need to call this anything but rhythm and cadence, something we hear and/or feel in the body, something we can use to develop a sentence that does its best work in the place it is needed in the essay or story.

In the above examples, I've employed the strategic tools of word choice and placement by varying sentences with phrases or clauses, adding richness through metaphor, enhancing tone and voice with fragments, and setting up pauses and providing emphasis with punctuation. In addition, I've noticed variation in rhythmic beats. One more thing some of us might use to good result, though I dare say not all of us are fans, is good old-fashioned seventh-grade sentence diagramming. As you might suspect, I happened to love that unit. Indeed, I've used it to understand difficult sentences in books I've read and, more importantly, I've used that handy little tool often to figure out a sentence I'm having trouble revising effectively. I suspect those of you who liked diagramming sentences are already using it in your revisions, but if you never learned or didn't enjoy it back then, why not do some reading now about that kind of visual processing of sentence structure? You might find it useful.

All these ideas and any others we can come up with are invaluable because paying attention to the plot of the sentence and to the needs dictated by the position of that sentence in the overall work will help us create the kind of interest and energy that gets the reader on our side, keeps the reader reading, and allows the writer to achieve that last crescendo and satisfying response in the reader, that good ol' *TA-DA!*

Exercise:

Re-plotting Sentences

1. Revisit the first few lines of your current work-in-progress and look at the plots of the sentences. Now, try rearranging the component parts in different ways and see what effect that has upon the tone, voice, mood, and on the content of the next sentences.

2. Rearrange the sentences below any way you like and go on to write the first paragraph.

a) *Yelling woke Corinne the night she ran away.*

b) *Bluebonnets bloom in the rain-washed sunset, a deep purple-blue carpet rolled out across the hill below our cabin.*

c) *When we all got settled again and the broken pieces tossed into the wastebasket, our teacher smoothed her hair off her forehead and looked at me where I sat minding my own business.*

d) *It was past dusk now, the woods across the road black and full of sound.*

e) *Her hair was all out of whack, pieces of the long part in back where it was lighter hanging over her face across the darker bangs, making her look as young and sweet as when he'd first seen her back in tenth grade.*

f) *The salt spray splattered and dried on my face; the taste of salty sea creatures lingered in my mouth.*

g) *She crosses the dining room turned fortune-teller's parlor, and passes through the curtained French doors into the living room.*

CHAPTER EIGHT

POETRY: "A MESSY BUSINESS"

What would happen if the wind blew in and swooped up all your well-ordered pages, tossed them to the ceiling, some even blowing away through the open window, and rearranged those that remained into a confused heap? How would you cope? Could you even begin to imagine that chaos as hopeful or even joyful? Maybe, if you took a step back and a calming breath, you might find a new way of looking and you might discover new treasures in that joyful heap.

In *The Art of Recklessness: Poetry as Assertive Force and Contradiction*, poet Dean Young says:

> [The writing of a poem] needs to be a messy business, a devotion to unpredictability, the papers blowing around the room as the wind comes in.

Unpredictability is linked to joy. Joy comes out of the unexpected pleasures of life, the flashes of insight, stunning metaphorical connections, and just the right words in contexts that elevate the ordinary to the extraordinary, the daily grind to unforgettable experience.

One of the many ways that my teaching life gets elevated from the ordinary is the unique way my MFA students respond to their reading. Recently a student who had engaged in a study of poetry that semester, and after reading Stanley Kunitz and Genine Lentine's *The Wild Braid: A Poet Reflects on a Century in the Garden*, said that the language and perception of the poetry and essays were "enough to fry the mind" and the images "to burn the retinas." What was so intriguing to her about these poems? What could make her feel the impact of the language and with such force that they ignited intellectual and emotional fire for her? It was the unpredictability, the surprise, the joy of the unexpected, and the use of those means to allow the discoveries made by the poet to foster discovery in the reader.

As poet Stephen Dobyns says:

> *It is always dangerous for the reader to think the poet is giving answers rather than seeking them. What we partly look for in a piece of writing is discovery. That discovery cannot be imparted, it must be enacted.*

This discovery, whether in prose or poetry cannot be imparted or dictated through content alone, but must be shown or enacted through poetic techniques, the music and shape of a poem, the sound and rhythm, the lines and stanzas, the white space on the page that takes the eye time to move across and thus provides the mental space between musical beats, the rests, pauses, crescendos, the echo of the last notes hanging in the silence.

W.S. Merwin, the seventeenth Poet Laureate of the United States, thought of poetry as akin to music with deep echoes in the human psyche through language and storytelling, saying, "It's close to the oral tradition. It's close to song."

With poetry, even when not read aloud, we pay attention to the music, to see how it is notated in the assonance and consonance, the line breaks, the enjambment of the line, the form and content melding into one, all its parts multiple and resonant.

So, what can you do in your writing technique to get the most of it, to make your work more than the sum of its parts? One important avenue for me, and one I would recommend to you, has been adding the study and writing of poetry to my work in prose. Not only has this enriched my writing life, but it has also introduced new ideas to me about what is possible in both prose and poetry. Nowadays, I see my ideas about poetry indispensible to my revisions of prose and vice versa. If you are a prose writer, consider a foray into reading and writing poetry as an enhancement to your skills. If you are already a poet, I hope some of my ideas about revision in poetry will be of use.

First of all, take time to play.

One enjoyable and useful activity is to let go of a rigid idea of order in your poetic lines and line breaks. Try mixing them up, moving them around, much like a fresh breeze through the window might do. Take scissors to your poems and slice them into lines, phrases, even single words that you can then move around, making from them new combinations that may lead you to a more powerful juxtaposition of idea and image.

Pay attention to the two most important positions in each line and see what you've got there. The most important position in each line is the last word and the second most important is the first word. If you read down the right margin, you'll most likely see some very strong image-filled words with good sounds that contribute to the tone and richness of a poem, especially, as we all know, in rhyming poetry. However, reading down the left margin can be almost as revelatory an experience. We can construct more interesting lines by making that first word as resonant as possible and employing other strategic means of lineation.

Enjambment means the carrying over of the sentence from one line to the next so that each line doesn't end with a period or comma or some other visual or aural stoppage of the line in the way that simple breath phrases might tend to do. Enjambment is one of my favorite areas to work with in revision as I try to avoid the monotone that end-stopped lines can produce. Also, you can use enjambment to create interest and to emphasize or undercut the ostensible meaning of the sentence in which the lines fall.

Mixing up the lines inside the stanzas can be helpful, too, even revelatory. We can also try switching around the stanzas to see if we can find more jump and surprise, more delight in that new ordering of the poem.

Keep the poem's syntax open as long as possible. You might find a treasure. If you haven't ever printed out your work and actually cut it up with scissors, give it a try.

As an example, I'm going to show you some of my revisions of a prose journal entry I wrote one bright rain-washed Vermont morning when I decided to use it to make a poem. This is only one possible way my poems might begin, but perhaps useful here as an example of one process a poet might use. Maybe some of these ideas can work for you.

I might begin with regular prose sentences or quickly written lines that are somewhat more like breath phrases, a kind of lineated prose, and then move to other lines that work on more than one level. Next, I'll break it into stanzas that have some integral interest of their own (as opposed to a kind of paragraph look and downward drive from top to bottom), and then decide whether to keep a left margin or utilize other locations in the space of the page. In my poems, I keep playing for quite a while, keep pushing for more electricity in the positions of the words and lines, still experimenting with different orders of stanzas or lines.

Now, to turn my quick journal entry into a poem:

1. Prose sentences:

Look at this morning, my love, this blue, blue sky, this sun. Oh, to dive deep into life, just like this, one moment taken to its very depths. Look at that—one drop of rain on a leaf, making rainbows.

2. Prose sentences broken into lines with a little revision:

Look at this morning, my love,
this blue sky, this sun.
Oh, to dive deep into life
like this, one tiny moment
taken to its depths,
one raindrop on one leaf,
rainbow colors prisming.

I removed one "blue," "just," "very," and "look at that," (all extra words), then added "tiny." I made the last two lines more rhythmic and graceful and found a word I fell in love with: "prisming."

3. Lines refined into free verse breath phrases:

Love, look at this morning,
this blue sky, this sun.
To dive into life like this,
one tiny moment
taken to its depths
one raindrop on one leaf,
colors prisming.

Here, in reading aloud I decided "Love, look" was more musical and a little less sentimental than "my love," which is also why I got rid of the "Oh," in the third line along with "deep," which was redundant with "depths" later on in the stanza and I had to choose between them. The same goes for "rainbow" and "prisming." As you can see, I was still loving that word, "prisming," even though I'd begun to realize it was a bit awkward to read aloud.

Next, I needed to break from simple breath phrasing and find more interesting and provocative line breaks.

Enjambment adds resonance and subtle undertones of meaning to each line so that the sentence can still be read and its apparent meaning apprehended, but a subliminal expression can also exist, shoring up or, perhaps, even undercutting the surface meaning.

4. Attention to enjambment:

Love, look at this morning, this blue
sky, this sun. To dive into
life, like this, one tiny moment
taken to its depths, one raindrop
on one leaf, prisming.

I made conscious choices about the little "packets" of information each line would deliver and how they might stand both inside and outside the sentence to build resonance of meaning. I also realized colors and prisming were pretty much the same image.

Now, I began to assess the visual effect of the stanza and didn't like how square it looked, how boxy and not at all evocative of the free feeling the morning had given me. I saw more could be done and broke the first two and last two lines into lines I liked better and produced a more organic rounded look, emphasizing that word I'd fallen in love with and thinking if it were on its own line, it might work better, be easier to say:

Love, look at this
morning, this blue
sky, this sun. To dive into
life, like this, one tiny moment
taken to its depths,
one raindrop on one leaf,
prisming.

5. Continuing to refine lines, cut extra words, juggle around line breaks, making it look even more raindroppy, playing around:

Love, look at this
morning, blue sky,
this sun. To dive into
life, one tiny moment
taken to its depths,
one raindrop on one
leaf, prisming.

6. The stanza still looked too tight, so I tried to open the poem by using more of the page. I also decided to give it a title and three stanzas in couplets:

love, look:

morning-blue sky
        sun   to dive into

one   tiny   moment
                taken to its depths

    one leaf   one raindrop
      a prism

    I deleted 'life', which had begun to seem heavy handed to me and too obvious, and '-ing' on 'prisming', a word that when I first found it seemed fresh and fun, but by this time had begun to appear too cute and called attention to itself rather than to the image I wanted to convey, and I had 'leaf' and 'raindrop' trade places so that the reader would see the leaf first then the raindrop upon it, then the prism colors.

    At this late stage, I might still be looking at word order and stanza and line order, maybe even trying for more logic and clarity using a title that states the circumstances or occasion for the poem. In this case, I added a title stating that this is after a rainy night. I even tried reversing the order of the stanzas and arranged the poem in a kind of leaning forward shape, as if the poem were about to dive off the page:

after night rain

        one leaf   *one raindrop*
               a prism

    one   *tiny*   *moment*
  taken   *to its depths*

    love   *look:*
morning-blue sky

sun   *life*   *to dive into*

I've heard it said that joy is the "pleasurable disruption of expectation" and in this process I don't mean only the expectation of the reader, but of my own expectations as the writer. I need to do something to disrupt my usual way of writing, my usual way of thinking and patterning. Doing something as seemingly strange and counterintuitive as reversing the stanzas surprised me and revealed the true feeling and meaning of this poem—at last. Also, as a side note, I strive to find strong words for the ends and beginnings of lines, but especially at the end of lines, and I mentally resisted the "to dive into" line ending throughout the whole process, sort of hoping to hide it if I couldn't figure out another way of getting rid of it. However, it finally showed itself to be the true pivot of the poem, not at the middle, but at the end, a dive into the white space of thought after the poem's end, I suppose. And, somehow, the word "life" came back and seemed to fit in a more practical and realistic way instead of what had become a kind of sappy, almost melodramatic way in the earlier revisions.

I hope my exercise of revision of this poem will whet your appetite for trying your hand at poetry if you haven't yet done so, or honing your skill if you are already writing poems. The solitary activity of discovery through poetry is wonderful for us as writers and as human beings. The insights we get through surprising ourselves are invaluable.

What we strive for in our stories and poems is to achieve a whole and finished work that is not just a sum of its parts, but a multiple of its parts, its form and content, exponential music. *From the paragraph to the sentence, from the line to the word, the most elegant arrangement will allow your stories and poems to become more than simply the sum of their parts.* Sometimes the most elegant is not the first discovered or the easiest or even the most regimented. Sometimes the most elegant arrangement of words on the page is the reckless one, the one abandoned to wind and intuition, where play and chance enter and rules become notions, and we each find our own best solutions when we are caught up in the joy of the "pleasurable disruption of expectation."

Exercise:

Poetry

These can be done singly, with a partner, or in a group. If you can, get into groups of even numbers, from 6 to 8. Choose a writing partner.

1. Do this portion alone:

Haiku: three lines in a syllabic pattern of 5-7-5. It might have a seasonal reference and a cut, an implicit comparison of two images divided in some way, perhaps by line or punctuation.

2. Do this one with a partner:

Tanka Renga: 5-7-5-7-7. The first person writes three lines—5-7-5, using original haiku; the second person finishes with 7-7 and begins next stanza with 5-7-5; continue to pass between you till poem is finished.

3. Group Poem:

Exquisite Corpse: Each person writes name on top of separate sheet of paper, begins with two lines, folds one back, passes to person on left, etc. till only three lines on page are left empty. Pass back to beginning poet who reads, finishes, and titles.

PART III

THE TEACHING WRITER

CHAPTER NINE

TEACHING: THE PROCESS APPROACH TO WRITING

I graduated from Vermont College's MFA in Writing the year before the MFA in Writing for Children and Young Adults was established. This was my attitude when I arrived in July 1994: "Just tell me what to do and I'll do it. I'm pretty smart. I'm certainly motivated. Tell me what to do and I'll do it!" In other words, I wanted step-by-step instructions and sure-fire rules to follow.

After the first workshop, standing under the Noble Hall portico talking with my friends, I might have said: "Is this a bizarre initiation rite into the field? Why are we doing this; why are we putting ourselves through this?"

Back home working through my advisor's comments on my manuscripts in successive packets: "Why didn't you tell me that from the beginning; now I'm having to do it a second and a third time! If you'd have just written that the first time I could have taken care of it and moved onto something else by now." But here's what I didn't yet know: This is a process, evolutionary, incremental, and unfolding. There's an ebb and flow to it and it turns back on you in unexpected ways, sometimes good, sometimes a bit scary.

This is the process approach to creative writing, an individualized, problem-posing approach rather than the old 'little teapot' method where the students sit passively while knowledge pours in, then they eventually pour it out again. Creative writing teachers are not looking to hand out a set of impersonal facts that first run through their impersonal teaching brains to become seeded in the waiting student brain-earth, facts that sprout as if by magic and bloom, producing a full-grown writer.

Here we're living, working, and writing within uncertainty and contradiction. We see that in the workshop setting where someone says one thing and someone else says a completely different thing. Even the leaders don't always agree. Wouldn't you think they might be embarrassed, that they could at least try to come to some consensus or whisper dissenting opinions to the student later? It all just seems so uncertain.

We writers, teacher and students alike, all of us in this together, exist in many kinds of uncertainties and many levels of unknowing. Like Keats, we strive to live with those doubts and mysteries that he wrote about as "negative capability" in a letter to his brothers back in 1817:

> ...(S)everal things dovetailed in my mind, & at once it struck me, what quality went to form a Man of Achievement especially in literature...I mean Negative Capability, that is when [a person] is capable of being in uncertainties, Mysteries, doubts without any irritable reaching after fact & reason.

The contradictions and uncertainties we learners see coming toward us all the time seem to be detriments; they seem to be roadblocks, but really they *are* the road. Vision/re-vision, creation/re-creation, work/rest, dialogue with persons (speaking to each other, maybe even writing in response)/dialogue with texts (reading and responding to those): these things transform us, transform our selves—and transform the world—and the words that we are trying to write.

The Spanish poet, Antonio Machado, tells us in "Proverbios y cantares": *"Caminante, no hay camino, se hace camino al andar."* ("Traveler, there is no road; the road is made as one walks.")

We persist with courage and discover our way as we go.

We walk into the dark and find the light, tread upon the rough ways and find a road. We learn by doing. We are here to give it our all, to teach, to learn, to read, to write, to grow, to become what is possible.

When we set out to learn something new, we know we will make many mistakes along the way toward mastery.

We will have successes and failures; that's how we learn. We need courage to exist in this kind of uncertainty as we find our way, lose our way, and find our way over and over again as writers.

The Swedish psychologist and poet, Tomas Tranströmer wrote of this "innermost paradox" in his poem, "At Funchal": "A drink that bubbles in an empty glass. An amplifier that magnifies silence. A path that grows over after every step."

The once clear path grows over and we lose our way. In a process that is both sequential and simultaneous, we find *and* lose our way as we make progress. We face the unknown and find a path to it through the known. In all we do, we live in uncertainty. We must lose the fear of it.

At Vermont College of Fine Arts, we use many of the methods that educator Nancie Atwell, winner of the first Global Teacher Award in 2015, demonstrated in her books, especially *In the Middle*, where she taught middle school students writing through the workshop process. With an emphasis on *dialogue*, she minimized her formal lecturing; in fact, she renamed them mini-lessons, in which she might spend five minutes at the beginning of a class going over a specific topic. She might also take the opportunity during workshop to do a mini-lesson, just to pause and spend a few minutes talking about some concept or question that had arisen. She found these mini-lessons more effective than a longer formal lecture because people best learn discrete amounts at a time, especially when the new ideas are encountered in action and practiced immediately thereafter. The old way of lecturing, as if opening up the top of the head like a teapot and pouring in or depositing information, is called the 'banking' approach and is about storing it up, saving it for something later. That's what formal lectures are designed to do. Students are supposed to be sitting in lecture halls with the tops of their heads open and the lecturer is supposed to be pouring things in. I have always liked lectures. It felt good to sit there open and ready to receive. It felt like I was learning so much, getting notes in my notebook. Maybe I was learning. A learner does need ideas upon which to reflect. Although the 'little teapot' method is what I often must engage in when I'm asked to talk about writing because that is the style of the room (lectern, microphone, white board, A/V aids, etc.), it is not the only possible mode of information transmission, and I love to be able to work in smaller groups where we can engage in a guided discussion and enjoy a full and open dialogue.

Another way we at VCFA engage in dialogue is through readings. When we have guest authors at VCFA, and we all want to go talk to them afterwards, that's part of the conversation of the text. When we have someone talking to us we want to respond. It's only natural. We have group and panel discussions in which we hear dialogue between not only the presenters and audience asking questions, but the panelists talking with each other along with the audience. The advisor/advisee conferencing that Nancie Atwell has with her classes, we also have at VCFA. We come to a residency, share a meal, take a walk, sit down together, and students plan their next steps in the writing projects, saying, "What do I need to do next?" Through our dialogue together we make guided, but individualized decisions about reading and writing in order to generate a semester study plan.

For some students this freedom and attached responsibility is surprising. Some might come to campus and say, "I've got to choose, I've got to figure out my own course of study?" Even with the guidance of the program's requirements and the aid of the advisor, it might take a while to get used to the idea, and they may think, like I did, "I don't even know if I trust this—just me and one other person?" At first, faced with this difference between our MFA and a traditional MA, I was surprised and somewhat shocked when I realized I didn't have the whole of academia hanging over my head telling me what I should read or what I needed to know—or think or believe—in order to enter the flow of knowledge and experience I needed to become a writer. At first, I didn't know what to do with all that freedom, but soon I came to see it as a function of my responsibility to myself and to my characters and their voices. That's when a huge wave of excitement and energy hit me, enough to propel me through the two years of MFA independent study and hard work into a life of teaching and writing.

Peter Elbow, Composition Theorist and Professor of English Emeritus at University of Massachusetts Amherst, former Director of the Writing Program, and author of a book on the process approach to writing, says:

If I feel some task as constrained rather than free, then I don't have to feel how much I care about it and fear failing. In short, I'm spared the risk of investment and caring. When choice is available, there is usually an initial resistance and tendency to do nothing at all. If this can be gotten past, if the choice of freedom can be fully assented to and the investment made, there turns out to be a liberation of energy.

I especially like the last part of this quote, that if you can assent to the freedom, take the responsibility that goes with it, and make the commitment to your own learning, "there turns out to be a liberation of energy." How many of us have felt that release of energy? When we give up the resistance, assent to the freedom, really care about it, when we engage in it, we can really go. At least for a time, then fears may creep back in and we stop and think, "Can I really do this? Is this working?" Just know that the tensions we feel and the fears that we have are part of the process. If you weren't in the process, if you weren't making progress, you probably wouldn't care and wouldn't fret over whether the work is 'worth it' or good enough, or what have you.

These tensions are built in when learning is happening, even though we all would like to relieve them. They come along with the investment and resultant energy release, partly because we, or most of us, haven't engaged in this alternative way of learning and teaching for a long, long time. Peter Elbow again:

> *When you allow real choice and self-motivated learning, the student reverts to the point at which real learning last took place. This often means going way back. They revert to what they really feel and think, not to what they normally produce in classes, papers, and tests.*

Some of us may go back to kindergarten or pre-K, the last time we learned by doing and by really engaging, or being immersed in language.

At VCFA, in addition to contributing to the field of children's literature through writing creatively, we read extensively in the field, highlighting, note-taking, marking, and remembering what we want to come back to, and then writing essays about literature. This response to what we've read is part of the dialogue. It's a conversation with the written word, the author, and with oneself. Dialogue also occurs in the letters written between student and teacher, between advisor and advisee. Students write about their discoveries, struggles, goals, and their advisors point out what they see on the page, and work on all aspects of writing, from small moments, word choice, and voice, to overall structure. This is all a part of the ongoing conversation.

The student readings are another kind of dialogue with an audience, as well as a type of publication. There's also informal conversation, the informal chat that's going on constantly inside the residency and outside it during the semester. The conversation continues at the next residency.

What we see at VCFA is students taking upon themselves the responsibility for their own education and sharing ideas in dialogue, both spoken and written, that will help others learn. The responses from the advisor are a large part of this process. The writer gets comments and suggestions from the advisor and the advisor continually learns how to respond to the writer and the text. We learn from each other—at least we should. It's a reciprocal action. Advisors are teacher/students and advisees are student/teachers; the process is dynamic and bi-directional, a two-way street. Ah, there's that road again, springing up as we walk.

Author and former VCFA faculty member Ellen Howard has said this about her experience of teaching the process approach to creative writing:

> *An astonishing thing I have found—although other life experiences have taught me this, too—is that I am completely convinced that I learn as much from the students as the students learn from me, so that although I thought I was going to be teaching, I find that I am a student in a way that I didn't expect.*

In effect, the student goes from unknowing to knowing and the teacher from knowing to re-knowing and even unknowing sometimes, both of them continually evolving and testing the knowledge and discoveries as they open before them, again and again, in new forms, new ideas forming into newer ideas.

This dialectical flow, the seeming contradiction of moving to and fro between uncertainty and certainty, shows up most definitely in the process of revision. On the same continuum between creating and editing, is the continuum of the intuitive and the analytical. Revision occurs along that continuum, constantly moving back and forth, back and forth. It's made up of the cognitive and the emotive, a flow between the two poles, moving closer to one or another at different stages of the work. Drafting and revision are *not* two separate operations, but one consisting of an ever-changing balance along that continuum.

We move between intuitive drafting and our conscious analytical work, moving back and forth. Reading as a writer to see how someone else solves the problem increases our understanding. Teaching is also this kind of dialogue. It's as simple as this, as author and former VCFA advisor Carolyn Coman says, "I'm a writer so I can talk about writing." We teachers-as-students and students-as-teachers are writers so we can talk about our notions about writing; we can all teach each other and learn from each other.

Paolo Freire, in *Pedagogy of the Oppressed*, referring to the banking theory versus the problem-posing theory (the 'little teapot' method versus the 'what if'—open-ended question—method), says that through dialogue the teacher and student become jointly responsible for the process in which both grow. He says that *liberating* education consists of acts of cognition not transferals of information. This harkens back to the tensions we all feel because, as Freire says:

> *Whereas banking education anesthetizes and inhibits creative power, problem-posing education involves a constant unveiling of reality.*

Even, perhaps, a reality we'd rather not see. But those things we may not want to see, we have to see.

> *The former (banking education) attempts to maintain the submersion of consciousness. The latter strives for the emergence of consciousness and critical intervention in reality.*

We have to think and wrestle with problems and solutions to become fully conscious beings. We have to emerge from this unknowing state we're sometimes in and see the world as it is and the self that we truly are, or are becoming.

We are always becoming and so are our stories. As we write we have the constant movement of our thoughts and our feelings, the images from the subconscious slowly, slowly rising up. There's no way we're going to get all we need into the first draft. It takes time because one draft teaches us the thing we need to know in order to write the next draft. And, unlike what I'd assumed when I first entered my MFA program, a student writer isn't going to get all the responses from the advisor that she might eventually find she needs on that early draft because it's a process for the advisor-reader as well. Even if something that will be commented upon at a later stage is there in the first draft the removal of the shades growing around it is going to make it more noticeable at a later stage. The dynamic movement of all these things ebbs and flows: our delving into the subconscious, coaxing it out, going back in, pulling it out. We're really good at tamping down the subconscious, but we finally have to allow the stories out, and the emotions of the stories out onto the page.

A friend of mine used to joke that writing was a kind of behavioral disorder. Well, in a way, he may have been right because you don't always act the same from day to day as you go through this process with a story. You change. Every time you go back inside your story and really revise, every time you enter your imagination and allow those things to emerge from the unconscious that are needed for the story, you will become a incrementally different person. Your own words will change you. Revision and the making of the self are interconnected. Maybe revision is even more liberating to the self than is the act of creating early drafts.

Freire says that problem-posing education affirms men and women as beings in the process of becoming, "as uncompleted beings in and with a likewise unfinished reality." So not only are we finishing ourselves, making progress in the growth of the self, as we move about within our stories, but also when we come back out and observe the world, our reality will have changed. Our actions impose themselves on the world and on our perceptions of the world as well. "Thus," Friere says, "to speak a true word is to transform the world." To name the world, you have to be in relationship to it. It's an act of creation, of love, of commitment, and of freedom.

Peter Elbow believes that:

Good new insights come. The process leads eventually to genuine decision where we feared we would stay becalmed forever in indecision, decisions which are usually richer and better than the options we originally vacillated among.

So trust it—you *can* trust it—this process. It's evolutionary: it's moving, it's growing. We're engaged in the exercise of becoming. It's contradictory. We even have contradictions within our own approaches to the process, which necessarily change over time, and we will have to find our own way somewhere along the continuum in order to be able to bring all parts of ourselves to bear upon the process, allowing the road to open up before us and close over behind us.

Everything is practice; life is practice: this is process. Practice is good. You learn as much from the things that don't work as those that do. Contraries that stump us, that we think are wrong, that we think are stopping us are not; they are making us go, giving us the push-pull we need in process to keep the tension tight enough to keep us going, to keep us learning-and-teaching, teaching-and-learning.

Exercise:

Dialogue with Texts, Other Writers

1. Do you make lists of books you have read and take notes to help you remember what each book was about? If not, start making such a list, but don't stop there. In addition to a sentence about the content of the book, write a couple of sentences about the technique you noticed most in the book, asking yourself:

a) What did the writer actually do on the page to bring about the effect I admire?

b) Is this a technique I might use in my work-in-progress?

c) Do I notice a problem in technique that I want to avoid in my own writing?

2. As a further exercise, practice what you have learned from your reading:

a) If you have noticed a technique you would like to emulate, revise a couple of paragraphs of your own work using what you've noticed.

b) If you have found something you'd like to avoid in your writing, consider what changes you would make and rewrite a paragraph or two from the book in question.

3. Do you have a writer's group? If not, you might consider looking for a compatible local or on-line group or class to join. Dialogue is good!

CHAPTER TEN

THE WRITING AND TEACHING LIFE

When I began to study creative writing, I entered a short story workshop where one of my first teachers prefaced her remarks about my story by saying, "A story should be capable of changing the world or saving a life." I was shocked. *Changing the world? Saving a life?* How could a story do that? How could MY story do that? I prepared myself for the worst, but then she added: "And this story is such a story." I was relieved, flattered, thrilled—but I didn't believe her. Not then. I do believe her now because simply through the act of making story, I have seen my *own* world change and the life I've saved may have been my own.

The intensive study of writing, the act of writing and revising, and eventually the teaching of writing have all worked together to change my life. Over the years I have been gratified to learn how the words I have written have entered my readers and changed them or their worlds, too. Because of this experience and my way of thinking about it, I am always eager to talk about the power of our words and the way our words can change us, how we, through the acts of imagining and revising, become the persons capable of writing the stories we are meant to write. Our writers' journeys lead us to places, experiences, emotions, and to people we've never encountered before. This isn't an easy journey and it's good to have an understanding teacher with high expectations along with you.

Stories that change and save don't have to be terribly intense and serious. Humor, even silliness can make a difference in a person's life and, as a result, in the world of that individual. They just have to be true. Of course, by *true* I don't necessarily mean *factual*. I mean true at the heart, honest and real, honestly written, honestly revised. No matter for what age you write or in what genre you write, your choices change you and your world, and maybe, like me, they may save your life.

I didn't intend to teach when I set out on my writer's journey. First of all, I didn't know how to write, so it didn't occur to me to imagine teaching others, but really, the main reason was that I wanted to spend my life writing. That's why I entered an MFA program—to learn to write. Not to learn to teach. Furthermore, no one in the program taught me explicitly anything at all about teaching. Most of the writers on the faculty were not only authors but also English teachers in colleges and universities around the country. They probably learned how to teach by the seat of their pants, too, and they spent no time talking about classroom teaching.

I did learn something about teaching anyway, as I listened to lectures and took notes, as I listened and participated in the workshops, as I wrote letters to my advisors and read their response letters to me, and as I engaged in further discussion with my classmates informally or as we read our stories to each other. I was learning about writing (that's what I was there for, after all), but also learning about teaching through observation of the faculty around me. They had several different styles, different approaches, different ideas and emphases. I learned that much of what they had to offer was their uniqueness, their own idiosyncratic approaches to the text. I also learned through osmosis the dialectical workshop method of teaching/learning writing.

When I graduated from Vermont College's Writing program, one that existed before the program in which I currently teach (the MFA in Writing for Children and Young Adults), and which concentrated on writing for an adult audience, I saw an ad in the Chicago Tribune for an opening at Columbia College Chicago in the English Department in Freshman Composition.

With some trepidation, I applied and got the job. I soon learned that a big bonus for me in teaching college-age kids, freshmen and sophomores mostly, was that they gave me ideas for my own creative work—they were young adults, some of them as young as seventeen. I really loved their personal essays and their journal entries, their stories and their poems, all with their own voices and attitudes and opinions, and their current slang. That's what I miss most now about no longer teaching young adults, the edgy newness of their kid-trying-to-grow-up voices and their recent memories of childhood and early adolescence. Columbia College Chicago, an arts and media school, is where I met my first graffiti and hip-hop artists, and where the idea for my Young Adult book *Trash* was born. I was inspired and challenged by the young people I was teaching in essay-writing classes and poetry workshops who wanted to be song writers, performers, serious avant-garde poets, filmmakers, or visual artists, and by the personal story of one young man who had broken his back in a three-story fall while running from police after writing graffiti high on a Chicago building. If I hadn't ratcheted up my courage and followed through with teaching, I'd never have found the story of *Trash*, and it probably wouldn't have taken the form of a long narrative in poems either. I found that I could write or revise something as short as a poem during the free-writing periods in my classes and it was good to write with my students, setting an example of what I was trying to foster in them.

My department's structure for writing classes was the workshop method with each essay going through three phases: 1. First draft brought to class and shared with two or three others in a small group for critique; 2. Second draft brought to class and shared with a small group and with me in a brief individual in-class conference; 3. Third draft finished and brought to class for reading aloud to the whole class.

If you have read writing teacher and theorist Nancie Atwell, you'll see that the structure used in my college was similar to that of her workshops. Another feature of my classes patterned after her ideas was the mini-lecture, a very brief, probably no more than ten-minute discussion of the assignments. This approach has as a key component dialogue, dialogue between people and dialogue with texts, both spoken and written.

Not everyone will teach in a college classroom, but most published writers will be asked to teach in one form or another. Often we are asked to do school visits in classrooms with the young readers of our books, often sharing with them ideas about writing poems and stories of their own. When authors are invited to do writers' conferences, say with Society of Children's Book Writers and Illustrators or other such groups of aspiring writers, they are often asked to give a lecture, lead workshops at the event, and do written critiques before arrival that usually will be followed up at the event with personal conferences.

These lectures might have a theme or topic that you'll be assigned, or you might be asked to talk about your books, your writing process, or your road to publication. Something to keep in mind is that most of the time your audience will be made up writers of varying levels of experience, interests, ages for which they want to write, and commitment to excellence. They will have different needs, goals, and understanding. Some of the questions you get will throw you for a loop. In a way, facing other writers takes more courage and versatility than teaching college students, or even your young readers.

Workshops in writers' conferences can be a challenge. At times, the level of dialogue can be quite high, but you may find that not to be the case all the time. Again, you'll be working with beginners as well as more practiced writers. Also, the emphasis on some occasions may fall more heavily upon 'fixing' the work before you and less on the whole writer, her future writing, and whole body of work. Sometimes the participants will be weighing their ideas and words carefully; sometimes, not so much. You may end up needing to tread with care or mitigate a difficult situation between participants. Not only knowledge and skill in writing are needed, but people skills, too. If you'll recall any workshops you've fully participated in, you'll realize you've gotten some people-skills practice already.

In many conference and workshop settings, the visiting author will be asked to do one-on-one critiques. That often means reading the pieces out of context and without knowledge of the writer's goals for her career or for the piece. You have to respond in your comments in as helpful a way possible, pointing out what you notice is going on in the writing and asking questions about structure, character, etc. When you meet with the writer, ask about intention and direction and anything else that will help put your response in a useful context, making any changes in your comments that might result from that new information. Sometimes the most important things you can do are listen and ask questions to help the writer feel more oriented toward her writing and her process, and become encouraged or cautioned for the work ahead.

People need to know they are being heard and might be more in need of talking out some aspect of their work than of hearing you talk about it. Many times the writer intuitively knows best what is needed, but cannot come to it without some urging, encouraging, attentive listening, and accurately reflecting what is being said.

Once your book comes out, you'll probably be invited to schools to talk with children or teenagers about your writing life. These school visits run the gamut from the author appearing in costume in character to poetry slams. What you do will be determined by your personality, the genres and subjects of your books, the age of the audience, and the requests or expectations of the host schools. Oddly enough, I've found that no matter whether I'm talking to elementary school age children about tornadoes and county fairs wearing a cowboy hat and surrounded by stuffed animals and sunflowers or to young adults about graffiti, poetry, and homelessness, the same messages come through and those are the themes of my own life. The themes of our lives tend to come forward in the course of our writing and in our teaching. I've found that my own large general themes have to do with persistence and courage and dealing with unexpected outcomes.

My life as a writer and teacher has certainly been an unexpected outcome. When I'm speaking to children and teens, I like to point out that most likely there are young writers in my audience, something that no teacher or guest speaker may have ever said to them before. In the time and socio-economic situation in which I grew up, that professional option was never mentioned to me and it took many years into my adulthood before I realized and believed I could be a writer—or a teacher.

Another type of school visit is the writers' workshop. While you may be asked to talk a bit about your own work, you'll be asked to lead a workshop for your young audience. I like to use poetry in these, partly because most youngsters haven't learned to dislike poetry yet and I hope to help fan a flame of love for it in at least a few of them, and partly because they can complete a poem in the time allotted. An example of how one poem can shape a person's entire life is that of my husband, Jerry, who still talks about the magic moment when his high school English teacher read T. S. Eliot's "The Love Song of J. Alfred Prufrock" to the class. This and another earlier experience of having a teacher read aloud chapters of the *Iliad* after lunch each day helped inspire him to become a librarian, an historian, a writer, and a voracious reader. In my own experience, poetry came into my life in a rush through a teacher's discarded *Sunset* magazine filled with poems about autumn. I don't know now whether the poems made autumn my favorite time of year or if my love of the fall of the year made me open to falling in love with poetry. I can still remember the way the edges of the pages curled up over time and the shiny lamination on the cover began to separate from the bright blue cover. Later, I entered the poems of Emily Dickinson so deeply that for a school project I spent hours drawing colored-pencil illustrations for many of them, imagining a world from her words.

One of my favorite writers' workshop school visits included all the Young Authors participants of a particular Chicago suburb along with their parents on a Saturday morning. After my assigned-by-the-organizer "inspirational talk" about being a writer, I divided them into groups and got them started playing Exquisite Corpse, a game I haven't had any group not have fun with, especially kids. At first the parents thought they were just going to observe, but I told them they had to play, too, and did they play! They all enjoyed it and the kids loved writing with their parents. Lots of laughter filled the room when they were reading their finished group-generated poems aloud to each other, then when it came time for each small group to appoint a reader to share one of their poems with the whole audience, a couple of the parents stood to read. Afterward, several parents came up, thanked me, and told me of their own desire to write while their young writers stood beside them with huge smiles on their faces.

Whether my talk did anything to inspire them, I'm not sure, but their own writing did inspire them to share with joy, both with their own children and each other.

Even when I'm not specifically asked to do a writing workshop, I like to get the group writing. At one school, when I had three different age groups to work with, I found that the lack of fear of poetry in the younger ages made them open to learning some things about poetry that the older ones seemed to find hard to comprehend. The feedback from the teachers was interesting, too, with the teachers of the youngest students wildly enthusiastic about some of the very same material that the sixth and seventh grade teachers said was too advanced for theirs. As odd as some may turn out to be, school visits can be greatly rewarding, especially when you feel you are able to make a difference in children's attitudes toward reading and writing.

You can find other teaching opportunities in blog posts, on-line classes and workshops, local community college classes you can design yourself, and in MFA programs. Prior to Vermont College's inauguration of the MFA in Writing for Children and Young Adults program in January 1997 there were no other graduate programs specifically geared to creating literature for young people. Now, there are several around the country and other sections opening in existing MFA in Writing programs. As teaching writers in colleges you will have opportunities to enter into a collegial relationship across institutional boundaries by joining your professional colleagues from other schools' programs in discussions of writing at professional conferences. Also, sharing information and knowledge along with other authors on panels at conferences such as those of the Associated Writing Programs, National Council of Teachers of English, International Reading Association, and many others, is another form of teaching that is highly rewarding.

Probably wherever you find to teach, the hallmark of a program's success will be flexibility and openness to new ideas and methods with innovative workshops and other opportunities for learning and participating. The goal of fostering real change person by person through empowering them as writers is paramount. As Paulo Freire writes in *The Pedagogy of the Oppressed:*

> ...(T)o speak a true word is to transform the world.
> ...Human existence cannot be silent, nor can it be nourished by false words, but only by true words, with which men and women transform the world. To exist, humanly, is to name the world, to change it.

As we write "true words," we transform ourselves, and the world around us. Writers "name" the world.

This freedom to name the world, along with the expectation of positive growth and change, is basic to our tasks as teachers and as learners. Especially if we aspire to change the world and save lives, or save the world and change lives, even if those worlds and lives we save and change are our own.

Exercise:

Saving Lives, Changing Worlds

1. Write about a positive change in your world as a result of something a teacher has helped you understand.

2. How might your art and the exercise of your craft change you and change others around you?

3. How would you approach a speaking engagement before a group of writers? Of your readers?

CHAPTER ELEVEN

"WRITE AT YOUR OWN RISK" EXCERPTS AND OTHER SHORT PIECES

In this chapter, I've collected a few of the short pieces I have contributed to the VCFA faculty blog, "Write at Your Own Risk," and for other occasions. Some are outtakes from lectures; some are personal responses to my life in the moment. One is a list of my own most frequent and persistent mistakes, a list one of my early writing classes asked me to compile, and a list that has turned out to reflect some of the same issues many of my students have wrestled with over the years.

I've included these here in hopes that my ponderings might strike a chord with you as a fellow traveler on the writing journey, and that you'll try some of the suggestions you'll find at the end of most of these.

Discovering YOUR Stories

As you devote your time to discovering the stories inside you and learning how to write them for your audience of readers, you will continue to build your skills and insights.

When exploring cause-and-effect, stimulus/response, action/reaction, try to:

1. Show impressions, fleeting sensation, and unnamable emotion rather than fully articulated statements;
2. Allow for confusion and changes of mind and heart;
3. Toss it all up in the air and let the reader catch it bit-by-bit, as mixed up and fragmentary as life and experience is in real life.

In revision, work on moving deeper inside, conjuring how it feels to have the emotion you ascribe to your character at the time:

1. Allow your experience, empathy, and memory to fill in the blanks;
2. Climb inside the character and see only what you can through those eyes, think only what that brain can

think, and experience the sensations of that particular adolescently volatile body;

3. Remember what you know about emotional dynamics and apply that knowledge to your characters' psyches, allowing, of course, for their own idiosyncrasies.

With every increase in plot tension there is a concomitant increase inside the character. In fact the build-up of tension inside the character determines when she makes a move that furthers the plot. A character has a problem she tries to solve, failing at first and thereby raising the stakes through successive tries and failures until the ultimate trial, which succeeds or fails, and thus ends the story. The most important thing at stake is what the character is risking that she holds dear, needs, or desires, and the story is really about the emotional turns the character makes in response to the incidents of the plot.

Events make no difference at all unless the character is moved in some way by them, unless the character's inner journey is the reason for it all. The reader needs not only to know what is at stake, but also to feel the life or death importance of it from inside the perspective of the main character. As events accrue and intensify, so must the emotional trajectory rise and peak, destabilize then find equilibrium in the end.

Proceed with faith in the writing process and trust in yourself as a writer. The very idea of an audience who wants or even needs what you have to give, that your words and the readers will finally find each other, takes faith. What else is life, anyway, but hope and faith, and doing what you are called to do with the greatest care and love you can muster. Love is given in *time*. Every minute that you work to get the words just right for that one person who might be waiting for them, needing them, is a gift. Time that seems selfishly turned inward—just you in a room with that blank sheet of paper or blinking cursor on the computer screen—is not selfish at all, but an expansive, and sometimes emotionally expensive, gift of self. This gift, from one human being to another through the vehicle of a fictional character come to life in all her emotional glory, has the power to show what only she (and you) can of the essence of being human.

Metaphorical Thinking

Peter Elbow, Composition Theorist and Professor of English Emeritus at University of Massachusetts Amherst, former Director of their Writing Program, and author of books on the process approach to writing, tells us that the sources of real learning are the ability to apply concepts widely and the ability to invent new concepts or to think in metaphors. When we make a metaphor, we start with two separate, seemingly unrelated, maybe even contradictory, things. We try to compare them, but see only their differences. In order to see how they relate to one another, we might try to connect them, not in a direct line, but by going through a third point, something entirely new. This is the triangulation of our thinking. It's usually through an abstract idea, maybe something hidden, at a place not readily available to us consciously where two different things are compared and the collision of ideas happens. As if by magic, it dawns on us what their connection signifies to us on a deeper level. We have a new, previously unimaginable idea.

The mind's ability to hold two disparate ideas at the same time is one of the things that make us human and this ability is the stuff of which metaphor is made. When two different things are held up side by side and compared, another new idea is born, one that springs from the intuitive and the emotive in a wild unruly, messy mix of cognition, *ignition*, if you will, where the emotive and the cognitive cannot be separated.

Metaphorical or analogical thinking, this acrobatics of the mind, brings about the new concept, usually at a higher level of abstraction. That's what we are going for, the new thing, a new understanding. From the comparison of two unlike things we arrive at something else, something that has as its attributes those of the original two made new in a third. Metaphors usually come into being when the emotional response is so intense that a simple direct statement isn't sufficient or when we are confronted with something new and for which we need new language for expression. To understand that something new we may have to have a new way of making connections, a new thought, a metaphorically created thought.

Here are some examples:

[Love] is an ever-fixed mark
That looks on tempests and is never shaken;
It is the star to every wandering bark,
Whose worth's unknown, although his height be taken.
(Shakespeare)

They say love is a two-way street. But I don't believe it, because the one I've been on for the last two years was a dirt road.
(Terry McMillan)

Happiness is the china shop; love is the bull.
(H.L. Mencken)

Love is a dog from hell.
(Charles Bukowski)

Juxtaposing two very different images can bring forth amazing new insights from our subconscious minds, contradictions that resolve into new concepts that partake of each of the original images, yet allow for greater depth of intuition and emotion.

Some time ago I heard the act of writing described as 'a ripe loneliness'—another contrary kind of description. Lonely is solitary, confined, and ripe is full, but we understand it because it tells us a third thing, it triangulates.

TRY THIS:
Make a list of nouns and cut them apart, shuffling and choosing two, then write a poem or paragraph that begins with "The _____ is a _____." See what simply juxtaposing two very different images can bring forth from your subconscious.

Action and Reflection

In our day-to-day lives as human beings we face many contradictions, dynamic tensions between things like the exercise of freedom and responsibility, non-verbal and verbal communication, words versus actions, or the relationship or seeming lack thereof between thoughts and feelings. But this is actually a dynamic movement between things, like moving from thought, into words and action, and back again.

It's a dialectic between action and reflection. In order to act we must think and if we think we will act. Paolo Freire, the Brazilian philosopher, educator, and author of books on critical pedagogy, says in *The Pedagogy of the Oppressed*:

> *In dialectical thought, world and action are intimately interdependent, but action is human only when it is not merely an occupation, but also a preoccupation; that is, when it is not dichotomized from reflection, reflection which is essential to action.*

Action and reflection: two sides of the same coin.

In stories, it is plot *and* character, motivation *and* event, seemingly separate processes, yet inseparable aspects that make up the whole. What the character does and says, the external workings—the things that we see—have to have reflection going on behind them; they have to originate in the inner life of the mind. There must be a dynamic movement between action and reflection, back and forth, because that's the way we are; that's how we work. Showing the inner workings of your characters' hearts and minds will go a long way in making your readers perceive them as believable and worthy of empathy and identification. Along this continuum between reflection and action at a balance point between them (and probably always in flux) is where we find our humanity.

TRY THIS:

As you develop your characters, consider how this essential connection between human reflection and action might relate to the characters you create in stories. How can you show this interplay of outward action and inner reflection in your current work in progress? Take a passage and revise with this idea in mind.

A Room of My Own

I've been looking forward for several months now to having "a room of one's own" to work in, to read in, dream in, just *be* in. Last May I moved into my new husband's house and moved all my furniture and boxes of books into his garage. In June the builders began work on a new addition that would also hold my study, be my workplace, and contain all my books. On Saturday night, they finished. I get to move in this week. My husband, a former librarian, will arrange my books and I will set up my desk, hang my pictures, and readjust my desk chair to just the right height. Ah, then I'll be ready for anything, right?

Right. And yet...

While it will be wonderful to have a steady place to go each morning to read my email and read student work, I've learned through this process that I don't have to be as chained to my desk as I once felt I had to be to produce my writing. Or maybe I should say I've been reminded of that. When I began writing, I did all my work in longhand on yellow legal tablets that I then revised once before committing the story to the computer. As I was typing it in, I did another revision, adding, deleting, changing, getting new ideas. That became my first full draft. Before I was ready to sit down at the computer, I wrote wherever I happened to be, in the house, in the yard, in the car, at my children's afterschool lessons. It was catch-as-catch-can and it was all I could manage back then. I printed out the revisions and took them with me, doing new revisions by hand on the printout, using the backs of the sheets to add or expand upon scenes.

Somehow, once my children all left home I came to the notion that I should sit at the computer and do all the work on it, revising the same document over and over there on the screen in front of me. I suppose I thought I was being more efficient. Maybe I was, but it occurs to me that maybe efficiency wasn't what I should have been seeking. Since May, I've worked on my writing and on my student packets during family trips to Arkansas, Missouri, D.C., and Italy. I've worked on airplanes and in airports, on guest bedroom beds, in baby's room rocking chairs, and even in the back seat on car trips. At home I've worked in an Adirondack chair on a shady porch, upstairs in a small attic room, and sitting in a lawn chair in the middle of a flowing brook with my bathing suit on and feet dangling in the water. I've written in longhand and on the laptop, in notebooks and around the edges of sudoku puzzles. I've also dozed and dreamed and gazed up into the blue and white of the Vermont summer sky. I am no longer chained to my desk. I love that.

So, here I am, excited about soon having this new room of my own, my computer back in its place on a real desk, my books in shelves made especially for them on the wall behind me, a view of rural Vermont before me. I will use that space, of course, but I hope I don't lose the mobility (and actual pen-on-paper handwriting) that I have regained in these months. I do want to lose the feeling of needing a particular book and knowing it is four boxes deep in the garage. I look forward to knowing exactly where it is on my shelf. I want to lose the unsettled feeling of having my life stored in the garage, but I don't want to lose the new/old freedom of writing in the world, writing about the real water running over my real toes, the real little fishes darting through the shadowed water, those little fishes only hints of the much larger ones well hidden in the shade of the rocky pools.

I hope I don't forget to let my mind wander, to doze, dream…and remember: I have met Eudora Welty two times in my life. Once in an otherwise empty hallway after a friend and I attended her reading at the University of Chicago; another time at a luncheon at the Southern Confederation of Writers in Chattanooga where she said she remembered me from the Chicago meeting. What a gracious lady! Before I met her the first time, I had read much of her work, but between the meetings I found THE EYE OF THE STORY in which she paraphrased something Virginia Woolf had said about making discoveries in subsequent drafts: "*The fishes get bigger the deeper you go.*" By the second meeting, I'd begun to understand what those two writing women meant and in all the years since, I've known I had to keep going deeper to find my real story and I've taught my students the same things. Funny what putting your toes into some cool brook water can do for your memory, your writing, your teaching, and your sense of the self you have become as a writer and a woman.

I hope this new room of my own never closes me in, but encourages me to wander, to dream, and remember. I hope it becomes the whole wide world.

TRY THIS:

Where do you write? Is it time to add some variety to shake your writing up a bit? Seek out a different place in which to write or another mode (pen instead of computer, for example) and see what happens.

Here Be Dragons: Placing the Story

For me, story begins with voice, a voice that fairly soon after I first encounter it, shows itself to come from a specific place. Once that place surrounds the voice, the character comes alive and moves in it. Without a location from which to speak, voice and character float away. Setting anchors story in a specific place and time, in sounds and textures, expectations and surprises.

On some medieval maps, dragons or other fantastical beasts were drawn about the edges, in the open sea, in the unexplored regions of the world. In that *terra incognita*, those uncharted, unknown lands, who knew what might lurk there? In those mysterious unknown climes there might dwell beasts, sea serpents, and even dragons.

What magic and mystery, what dragons and surprising creatures have come into our lives and become real through story! Think for a second of these places: Narnia, Hogwarts, Treasure Island, Cold Comfort Farm, Mr. McGregor's Garden, Earthsea, Goldengrove, Camp Green Lake, Jordan College, The Garage on Falconer Road, Middle-earth, The Underneath, The Night Kitchen, at Sea in a Pea-green Boat, The Hundred Acre Wood, Toad Hall, a Raft on the Mississippi River, Sleepy Hollow, the Boat with Two Wise Eyes on the Yantze River, Outside Over There, Wuthering Heights, a Kingdom by the Sea, The Forest Primeval.

THIS is the forest primeval. The murmuring pines and the hemlocks,

Bearded with moss, and in garments green, indistinct in the twilight....

When my youngest daughter, Stephanie, was only about three years old and her older sisters around six and fourteen, their father and I took them camping high in the Sangre de Cristo Mountains between the Spanish Peaks and Trinchera Peak just below Bear Lake and Blue Lake in Southern Colorado. The Cucharas Creek burbled alongside our tent site and branching trails led through the forest up to the lakes past beaver dams that formed smaller ponds along the way. We'd hiked high into the glacier valley when, just after noon, a thunderstorm rumbled in over the mountain. We ran for camp, father and two older sisters faster than the three-year-old and I could go. As the thunder got closer Stephanie and I entered the wooded part of the path with the others far ahead. Soon we lost sight of them and at the fork in the path stopped to try to figure out which way they had gone. I knew that both paths ended up back at the campsite, so we took off along the left-hand path. Soon we could see a bit farther along and the rest of the family was nowhere in sight.

Stephanie wanted to go back and take the other path, but I told her, "This path will end up right where we started. You'll see just as soon as we get out of the forest."

She stopped still and pulled back on my hand. She moved close to me and gazed all around at the huge looming pines and into the dark patches of shadow, fog, and mist between them. "Is this the forrrrresst?" she said. Her little eyes reflected all the mystery, magic, and terror of all the fairytales she'd heard by that time in her young life.

We were in THE FOREST and who knew what dragons, fairies, gnomes, witches, and other beasts of *terra incognita* might meet us along our path? Thunder and a little rain were nothing compared to the adventure we entered in that moment when physical "real" place intersected with story. I have to admit that through her reaction—and her imagination—that wooded path became THE FOREST for me, too, and transformed into something more magical and a little more terrifying than it had been when it was just a real place on a real mountain in very real Colorado thunderstorm. It was as if the glaciers had reformed behind their mounds of stone rubble and reabsorbed the lake water back into themselves. The wind blew colder and the rain turned to sleet and we entered a time long lost to the others on that mountain. We were in the forest primeval.

As writers, we sometimes think of setting, as Eudora Welty calls it in her essay, "Place in Fiction," in THE EYE OF THE STORY, *"one of the lesser angels that watch over the racing hand of fiction,"* but she also says:

> *...so irretrievably and so happily are recognition, memory, history, valor, love, all the instincts of poetry and praise, worship and endeavor, bound up in place. From the dawn of man's imagination, place has enshrined the spirit; as soon as man stopped wandering and stood still and looked about him, he found a god in that place; and from then on, that was where the god abided and spoke if ever he spoke.*

In our stories, setting and place are determined by character and character's reactions to them. Character is affected by place in a wholly and even, perhaps, holy way. Voice-character-place, bound together, inseparable, where the god abides and speaks, if ever she does speak.

TRY THIS:

How does place affect the voice of your characters, their attitudes, and beliefs? How might you incorporate details of place more fully in your writing? Make a list and revise a passage of your work accordingly.

Family Life and Writing

Family. That's what I'm thinking about these days. My own growing family, of course, as it expands through marriages and births, but also my students and their families as they juggle and sometimes struggle with the demands of the MFA program and ongoing family life. They have had to set up new schedules of work that sometimes impinge upon the other members' needs and wants. They sometimes have to persuade the other members of their families—and sometimes themselves—that this writing for young people is serious business, real work, and, surprisingly, not particularly easy.

Recently, I had an email from a former student whose baby was still under a year old and who worried about her need to write and her need to mother and how to reconcile the contradictions between the two. I don't know that I have an answer for everyone, but I do know that in my own life I've had to come to the realization that I just cannot do it all. At least, not at the same time. There are times for writing and times when writing has had to take a back seat to life when I've had to simply live through the events, some happy, some sad, and some just darn hard work. I've railed against the interruptions, worried about managing everyone's needs responsibly, argued against unreasonable demands, allowed myself to ignore important other things, allowed myself to ignore my characters' voices, and even, at times, decided that for a certain period of time I wasn't a writer. My children got ill, they sang in concerts, danced in recitals; they married, had babies, adopted children. For me, these years have seen a divorce, a teaching career to begin, a parent's illnesses, several moves, remarriage, and a new house to build. As Tim Wynne-Jones wrote in a recent Write At Your Own Risk blog post: "Sometimes the well runs dry and you need to let it fill up again." I can attest to that! Between all these things in life I've learned that the writing returns, the stories unveil themselves, the characters yammer away again. Sometimes they form up into novels, sometimes into picture books, but always, for me, there are poems. When I do as Coe Booth urges in another blog entry and "commit to sit," my meditations open up for poems. When I have the courage to love what I love, as Julie Larios urges her readers to do in her recent blog post, poetry is there.

For me, all along, that has meant that when I do love my life, when I take the time for my children, when I take time to grieve what grieves me, and love what loves me (and I love), then poetry is there, story is there, writing is there, waiting—and even when I'm not producing pages and pages a day, I'm still a writer. When there's silence in the igloo, that doesn't mean the wind isn't still blowing up a storm outside.

Of the many things I've learned from my students and my own teaching and writing life is that it is rare for two of us to have anything like the same writing process We each have our own ups and downs, our own enervating experiences, our own dramas. We have our own places of peace and ways of meditating. We are not the same; our stories are not the same.

If we can honor our differences, learn our own pathways, and allow ourselves to live our lives as they unfold, really live them, honestly and without guilt about what we "ought" to be doing, we will cut out a lot of the anxiety and stress so many of us suffer. If we stop worrying about whether we are disciplined enough or dedicated enough or even whether we'll have another story to tell, then we might see life's interruptions and demands as a part of our own creative process.

CONSIDER THIS:
What do you need to do in your relationships and writing life to find the balance you need at this point in your journey? What steps can you take to create that balance? What requests do you need to make of others? What do you need to ask of yourself?

S.W.E.P.T.: Making a Clean Sweep

I grew up in a family where once we started a project, we stuck to it to the bitter end. My dad spent many entire weekends overhauling our cars' engines. My mom could make a dress in a day, even if it took her past midnight and into the wee hours of the next. My sister and I always had chores to perform and we had to get them done on the day they were assigned. I have always thought that was how a person got things done; you got up, got started, and kept on till you finished. Even our scout's honor code included: "Remember to finish what you begin."

I understood why such a caution was important, and even a part of an honor code, because, as I learned once I grew up and set about starting my own projects, if I didn't persist to a rapid finish, I would clutter my sewing and art cabinets with unfinished projects, projects that lacked their original luster once I had set them aside for a considerable time. This happened with my writing, too. Many of those at first exciting projects were never finished. Through those failures I learned that I needed to work fast before time grew short and my enthusiasm faltered. That meant staying up way too late reading the library book due the next day. That meant allowing my daughters to stay up way too late to finish that overly detailed poster for school the next day. That meant being a tired-out family way too much of the time.

Time management for me back when I was raising my three daughters was constrained by the hours of school or extracurricular lessons and activities. I had to fit everything that needed doing into the few and small time slots available over the course of a busy family's week, which was not the way I naturally worked. Most of the time, things didn't fit smoothly and, many nights, I stumbled to bed in the wee hours only to have to wake up early to get everyone ready and out the door.

Then came the time when my daughters were grown and I was divorced and living alone. I could do anything any time I wanted. I could paint the basement all night long or read all day or write for hours and produce pages and pages of material, exhausting myself with the continual drive to *finish*. Or I could sleep late and sit around gazing out my windows at the Vermont mountains for hours. There was no such thing as a rigid and set schedule. I let my enthusiasms and my exhaustions lead the way. I got quite a bit done, but I also amassed a few unfinished projects, and never felt the kind of balance I longed for and thought I'd find once my schedule was up to me and no one else.

Enter the next phase of life: A new marriage to Jerry, a former librarian, who retired early and had been retired for a few years when we met. By then he had established his routines to fit his own daily rhythms. He told me early on that he read in the mornings and listened to music in the late afternoon—those were not negotiable activities. That sounded fine to me, so we began our life together, Jerry with his slow mornings, me with the learned need to get an early start on whatever project with which I'd become enamored or shamed into doing, whether it was cleaning the bathrooms, painting a piece of furniture, or starting a new book.

While I continued my usual fits and starts kind of progress, I noticed that Jerry was getting lots and lots done in a day. He might read nearly all morning, but afternoon found him doing little chores, just a bit of something here, something there. I noticed this most when a huge load of firewood seemed to get split and stacked with only a half-hour here or an hour there each day. I would have worked at it all day, day after day, till completion and I'd be a wreck, sore muscles and nicked fingers. I would have hated it, and I would have hated that it took me away from other things I wanted to do. Jerry relished getting outside every day and watching the stack move from a jumble on one side of the wood area to fine tall stacks ready to burn on the other. He might take a long walk or a bike ride that same day, do some repairs or paint a section of the house, then come in, listen to music, and enjoy an evening knowing he'd accomplished a lot. Still having things I needed to do, I often felt frustrated with my day.

That's when I decided to make a clean sweep of it and change my low-down ways. I'd copy his process and make myself move from one task to another throughout the day and not get so narrowly and intensely focused, which too often resulted in tiredness, boredom, feelings of self-pity, futility and frustration. I analyzed what I needed to do to make my life what I wanted it to be, balanced and productive—and satisfying. I came up with this anagram, S.W.E.P.T., for all those things I wanted to do in a day, but usually got derailed from by another activity. I wanted to get more physically fit, get more writing done, and manage my household tasks and projects.

Here's my new daily regimen:

S=Stretches—I loved yoga and ballet classes when I was younger, especially the stretches, so I have incorporated a short time for waking my body up with stretches into my mornings.

W=Work—This makes up the largest portion of my days. I include reading, writing, and teaching in this, with emphasis on my own reading and writing time when I don't have student work to read, and on reading and commenting upon their work during the seven to ten days we call "packet week." I tend to do my reading and commenting on student work in the morning and do my own writing in the afternoon. I have finally stopped trying to make myself a morning writer when it obviously isn't in my circadian rhythm. I've also found I get more writing done when I'm not focused on getting a lot of writing done. I'll never forget hearing Kate DiCamillo in a visit to VCFA say that she limits herself to two pages a day, but keeps up that steady pace as she forges ahead daily on a new manuscript. I can't make myself stop after two pages, but I don't attempt to wring the most words I am capable of out of a days' worth of writing. I like the way that placing some limits on each day's production, makes me more ready to sit down the next because I know where I'll start and am eager to get it down on the page.

E=Exercise—Biking, walking, hiking, canoeing, skiing, dancing. Exercise will slip out of my daily schedule unless I'm very disciplined, but the more regular I am with exercise, the more I miss it when I don't manage to find time for it. I've learned I need to prioritize exercise in the day or I allow time to slip away.

P=Projects—These are long-range tasks that I'm learning to break into smaller chunks to accomplish. For example, I spent a couple of months last winter organizing old photographs and filling new photo albums, something that I'd delayed doing because I thought I'd have to do it all in one huge energetic burst. I found out that what I really needed was time to enjoy or grieve as I remembered the precious events and people in my past.

T=Tasks—These are short term and usually recurring jobs, like cleaning or grocery shopping, and tend to take over too many of my days. Rather than exhausting myself by cleaning all day until everything is clean all at the same time, I've found that breaking down the tasks to a couple per day makes the whole thing not so daunting.

What I've written above and it sounds so ordinary, not life changing at all, but these changes have made a huge difference in what I've been able to accomplish in the last year. However, the most important part for me has been the satisfaction that being a more balanced person gives me. I'm a writer, but not only that; I'm a teacher, wife, mother, friend, and many more things. I am not satisfied with being only one thing in my life; I want to explore and grow and not feel I'm robbing one important part of myself to fulfill another.

I don't always get every one of these things done every single day. There are still times when one area overtakes another and I've given myself that flexibility. For example, I still have a hard time getting myself to exercise daily, but sometimes we take half a day for a hike or a canoe trip. I figure it balances out over time, and that's what I'm looking for—balance.

Have you *S.W.E.P.T.* today?

TRY THIS:

Set up your own S.W.E.P.T list and put your new schedule into practice for a week. Then assess and see what changes you want to keep and what else you might want to include in order to gain balance in your life and your work

Sharon's Top Five Writing Mistakes

1. Forgetting that the real story is discovered through revision.

2. Not keeping the imagination fully engaged through every stage, every revision, even in the final stages.

3. Trying to "fix" the words.

4. Not keeping the character's state of mind (POV) available to reader at every turn.

5. Not being willing to "go there" emotionally.

PART IV

IMAGINATION, REVISION, AND SELF-MAKING

CHAPTER TWELVE

WHAT DO YOU THINK YOU ARE DOING?

A few years ago, I was a guest for several days during the Vermont College of Fine Arts MFA in Visual Art residency. Now, I find that I am often reminded of the visual artists' statements that I read during that time. Those statements dealt with not only the media employed, but also the motivations and origins of the work produced. In the critiques, after the exhibit had been viewed and discussed by other students and faculty, the artist had a chance to answer questions and to talk about the reasons, means, and objectives of their art. Often this involved consideration of what they'd done in the past and what they hoped to do in the future.

This got me thinking. I wondered if we writers might benefit from writing artist's statements ourselves. If so, what could we say about our writing that would clearly state what our aims are both with our craft techniques and with the content of our stories and poems?

Can you write a statement that takes into account where you've been in your writing life and where you would like to go, and where exactly you are right now? Can you investigate your motivation for writing in general and for each story in particular? Have you thought about the themes of the stories you've written? Can you identify a thematic thread that runs from one writing project to another? What does that thematic thread say about you, about who you are, where you've been in your life's journey, where you are headed, and whether that is your intended destination? Are the themes similar or varied?

In grappling with these questions I found myself remembering my own life's journey and pondering what makes for fulfillment in life, things like having a sense of purpose, dealing honestly with ourselves and others, living in relationship with others, having satisfying work to do, and finding happiness in the large and small things of life.

Purpose

When we truly believe we have a purpose in life, whether vague or urgent and specific, we may feel the pressure to make some kind of change in our lives so as to be true to ourselves and live as our authentic selves. Many of us go on to further study, whether formal or self-directed, in order to discover our paths to authenticity and to equip ourselves for the journey. We set forth on a quest. Twice a year, new students step through the doors of Vermont College of Fine Arts on their new quests, mustering the courage to discover and begin to fulfill their purposes in life.

A few of the younger students forge a fairly straightforward path from earlier education through graduate school to a writing career, but many, many of us have wended our meandering ways through other careers, other attempts to find our authentic pathways, other lives. I have watched these younger students with a kind of awe. How did they know so soon that writing was their calling? Of course, I know that some of them will do as I have done, as many of you have done, and find other paths and other purposes as their lives progress. Still, I envy them in a way. I was already in my forties when I entered my MFA program and only since then have I felt that I have found my own true pathway in writing, getting some stories, essays, poems, and books published, and in teaching writing.

How about you? Have you found your true purpose, the one that allows you to express your authentic self in the world, through your writing? What *do* you think you are doing, as a writer and as a person acting in the world? Why do you do what you do day in and day out? Are you able to do what you desire and intend with your life?

What helps and what hinders you? Keep the things that help and see about reducing or losing those things that hinder.

Honesty

We think of writing as a way of expressing ourselves and our feelings, and it is, but has it become a shield or alternative to authentic expression in our everyday lives? It's easy to bury ourselves in our characters' psyches and emotions and insulate ourselves from our own need to interact and express ourselves to other real live walking-talking human beings, and their need to be in relationship to us in that way. On the other hand, delving into our characters' deepest needs, desires, and responses can make us more empathetic human beings. It can open us to the world around us and to the people we encounter every day. Are you finding a balance between the two? Are you allowing your work to teach you how to live a better, more genuine life?

Relationship

Writing is a solitary endeavor, so what regular routines have you set up to keep in touch with friends? A writing class or conference is a great way to do this, keeping one foot in the work and the other in a bit of the social life that feeds it. We need this, but we also need to keep the doors of friendship open to our non-writer friends or to that singing group you have joined or the painting class or faith community or political action group. We need to stay open to as many avenues of life as possible and to those people who are truly friends. Of course, this also includes the friends who are our families, our loved ones, those we need and who need us. Staying open and staying involved feeds us as people and gives meaning and depth to our writing lives.

Happiness

How does happiness manifest in your writing life? Even if accomplishing your complete goal for one day is thwarted, what about allowing yourself to celebrate the work you do get done, even if it isn't as much as you had intended? What have you accomplished in the face of life's other encroachments? Sometimes, even when we have a good solid writing day, we still beat ourselves up for the day before that didn't work out so well or worry about the next day's possible failures instead of honoring the work we did get done. Honor it, celebrate it, and you will be more likely to repeat it the next day.

If the work you do isn't making you happy, it's time to reassess either what you are doing or how you are doing it.

Work

Our work can bring us happiness, if we allow ourselves to truly experience it, to take pleasure in even our smallest triumphs. However, too much of the time, work is just work, hard, not fun, occasionally debilitating, and sometimes isolating. They say that writers should write from experience, so when do you get that experience? Is it all remembered or extrapolated from old experiences, historic, a nostalgic, often melodramatic walk down memory lane? Or is it mostly derived from current entertainment, movies, TV, popular fiction? What if getting out in the world and experiencing something new *is* the work? What if experience is the fodder for imagination? What if writers need to have alternating periods of intensive writing and intensive living? This isn't a nine-to-five job; it's a 24/7 one, and no one can sit at a computer all day and all night every day and every night. If sitting at the computer for hours and hours and staring at the blinking cursor isn't working for you, get up and go outside and go somewhere or do something. Live a little.

Questions for Reflection

Beyond self-expression, *why* are you doing what you are doing? Do you want to change lives? Do you want a career, to find a purpose in life and to get paid for it—how great is that? Do you desire fame, need a place to belong in the world, or a way to establish your identity? Writers write for many different reasons and over the course of our writing lives, our dreams, motivations, and needs may change. Sometimes forward progress seems magical, but other times we may falter. Sometimes we doubt ourselves, while other times, we ride our stories to the clouds.

What encourages you? Discourages you? How do you keep going through it all? How do you find a balance in life—career, family, spiritual practice, health matters? Do you struggle with inner conflict, with guilt or fear? Or do you struggle because of outside expectations and others' needs?

What exactly are your goals? What steps do you need to take to accomplish them? What celebrations do you enjoy when you have done what you set out to do? On the way to the large goal and large reward do you reward the success of the small incremental steps that must be moved through to get there?

How can we recognize and name success when it might not look like what we first imagined? How can we celebrate who we are and what our unique selves have contributed to our world in the face of the puzzling ups and downs of our chosen profession? How do we manage the hard work and yet, at times, the surprising ease involved in the process? How do we reconcile the encouragement/discouragement rollercoaster that comes with the ever-changing demands of writing and publishing our work for children and young adults?

How do we sustain ourselves? How do we hold onto our resolve, our courage, and our joy? What happens if the joy disappears?

I can ask all these questions because I have asked all of them in my own writing life, and many more besides. Things like:

Do I quit now? After all it's been 12 years that I've attended SCBWI meetings and taken part in workshops and conferences and I still haven't sold a book.

Okay, I quit.

And I did, actually, quit. Several times in my first dozen years of writing, but that lasted only a few months at the most and I was back with my characters, back with the words on the page, living in language and imagination. Finally, I realized and accepted that this was my life's assignment when new characters' voices came into my head and their predicaments made their way into my heart. I found I couldn't resist following along to find out what might happen.

When did you become so connected to words on the page that your future seemed destined to involve writing them yourself?

I was a child whose first career aspiration was to be a cartoonist. I drew pictures constantly and lived in my imagination in those pictures and in the stories I made up about them and in other stories I heard read to me, and later, those I read to myself from first grade into adulthood. I revered writers and teachers, but never thought I could be either. Why? Probably because I saw no one in my family or my family's associates doing either. Being a teacher was only a little less out of reach than that likely imaginary (or dead) personage, the writer. What's more, in my world, the most influential, if not most educated person I knew was the preacher in my church. Little boys in our denomination were encouraged to take up preaching as soon as they could read, hold a Bible open in one hand, clip on a tie, and grow tall enough to see out over the podium. Little girls might aspire to marry one of them. I was a little girl who wanted to *be* the preacher, but knew I had to settle for being the preacher's wife. Oh, well, a preacher's wife could be the Ladies' Bible Class teacher when her husband wasn't available himself on Wednesday mornings. In order to do that, she would have to read and study and become educated herself and that appealed to me.

Soon education itself became my goal, and in college I vacillated between study for careers of service in the helping professions (social worker, psychological counselor), in biology, and art. I kept coming back to visual art, but finally decided I wasn't talented enough to pursue it as a vocation. It would have to be my hobby. I didn't yet understand about growth in proficiency through practice and revision. I also took as many electives as I could in literature, enough to make a minor when my major finally became psychology. I seemed to need to read outside my field during each semester as a kind of escape. Literature classes gave me the excuse, but also the responsibility to read and do my writing assignments. They were for a grade and, for sure, I had to keep my grade point average up. I had too much pride and way too little money to do otherwise.

In giving you this recap of how I grew into a writer, I hope to jog your memory about the paths you, too, have traversed to get to this moment. We may have forged different or similar paths, followed different or similar dreams, but we are writers dedicated to writing good literature for young people, all of us in this together, in it for the long haul.

Think about where your path took you on its way here, to this day, to the words you are writing, the stories you are living in your imagination, the characters whose voices call to you. You may have come to writing by a more direct and shorter path than I did; others of you took more time to get to this place we share. Odd isn't it that we share so much experience as writers and yet our moments of true inspiration and hours of intense writing and revision are solitary? That's why we need to hear each other's struggles and triumphs, to come together, to tell each other our stories, to give each other strength.

A bit more of my story: I graduated from college ten years after I graduated from high school. I'd had some interruptions, gotten married, had a premature baby who was deaf and who required a good deal of extra parenting time and attention for many years; also, whose hearing aid training and speech practice enabled, indeed, required, us to spend a lot of time in children's books together. What a revelation that was to me. Children's books had so much to give to my child who needed so much. Those stories also gave so much to a young mom who didn't know what she was doing. They also represented what I'd loved for so long, art and literature combined, similar to the work of a cartoonist, an art form that wrapped up pictures and words and ways to teach and help all in one small, sometimes silly, package. You'd think I might have glimpsed a future for myself in that work, but I still did not. I didn't have a solid background in reading good literature for children. My family had only books we could buy in the check-out line of the grocery store, so how could I even begin to write for kids? It never even occurred to me.

I went back to college to prepare myself to become a clinical psychologist. But in my very last semester I had an open slot for an elective in my schedule and I took a leap and enrolled in a writing class. That may have been my first inkling that I wanted to do this work, but I took it more as an escape class so I could read just as I'd done in the early years of college. We could write anything, but I found myself writing word sketches in poetry, something I'd never have thought to do before. In fact, I didn't really think of them as poems but as simple and quick responses to the exercise prompts. The professor told me I had something special and I should keep writing. I didn't take him seriously. He was a known flirt and I thought that was what he was doing. Just flirting with me.

Years went by, two more daughters came along, giving me many happy hours filled with reading children's books. My oldest daughter discovered young adult literature and we exchanged and discussed the books she was reading. In fact, I was introduced to Norma Fox Mazer and many other wonderful writers through a book in my deaf daughter's hands. By then, good children's literature was fully a part of my life, helping me live it, and helping my daughters grow up. But writing still wasn't something I'd thought of doing.

How about you? When did you know that not only did you want to write, but that you wanted to write for young people? Some of you may be able to point to the Society of Children's Book Writers and Illustrators, as I am, to find the generative spark that got you going and the support that allowed you to become serious about writing and to take yourself seriously as a writer.

When my youngest daughter was two, I ran across a small ad in the Fort Worth Star-Telegram announcing that Joan Lowery Nixon would be speaking at a Society of Children's Book Writers' luncheon. That turned out to be the formative meeting for the North Central Texas chapter of SCBW (they hadn't added the "I" for Illustrators yet). I was fascinated and, besides, they needed me to help this thing get going. We met again and with only about seven people attending that day, we got the chapter off the ground. All of us had to take on leadership roles, so I got busy organizing—and I got busy writing. I wrote picture books that were exhilarating to work on, to try to make better, to share with others who were doing the same thing. I found I loved writing, loved revising, loved my fellow writers, and for the first time felt I really belonged in a group outside my family or my church. They got me and I got them. I reveled in belonging to a Writer's Circle.

The next step was deciding I wanted to be and, if I were lucky, could be published. That was a huge step. That implied a career path, a potential way to make some money while staying at home with my children, which I'd decided I truly wanted and needed to do, at least till my eldest finished school. By then she was developing into a wonderful student, a good writer herself, but navigating mainstream schools with no deaf interpreter services was exhausting and often confusing, so I needed to be as available as possible. What an ideal profession I had found—doing work I loved and working from home.

Have you felt this, too? What a relief to be able to work on your own, at your own pace, free to write whatever and almost whenever you wanted. To be your own boss and, if needed, care for family concerns at the same time. And even more exciting, to come to believe you had a real chance to see your stories in print, between book covers, lovely art added, on bookstore shelves, in reader's hands. Your ideas carried by your own words into young readers' minds and hearts. What an exciting prospect!

So…I sent manuscripts out. Far too early. I sent barely formed stories to famous editors and illustrious houses. I sent amateurish poems out to the best literary journals, even to the New Yorker. (I still blush at the memory.) I got back terse rejections slips, bits of paper I became inordinately proud of. They proved I was a writer, a serious one, a busy and happy, if rejected, one.

Did you go through that phase, too? After a while, though, I began to get little handwritten notes or even entire sheets of paper with a request encouraging me to try them again. I was thrilled. I tried them again and again, but after many near misses and despite those few encouraging letters, I decided I needed to go back to school—in another field. I attended Texas Christian University's Brite Divinity School for a while with a plan to work in pastoral counseling in hospitals and hospices. This was right after my dad had died from cancer and I'd begun to feel that I was not doing something of real import in the world. I wanted to make a difference. I remembered that I'd once studied biology and hoped to do cancer research, and now I wondered if somehow I could have made a difference in the outcome of my father's disease. Guilt had gotten to me.

Soon after this, we relocated to a suburb of Chicago for my husband's work and I couldn't continue with my theological studies. Although I'd quit writing, I felt the tug again and soon returned to an old manuscript entitled *Great-Aunt Thelma's Buggy Ride,* which eventually became *Old Thunder and Miss Raney.* I went to an SCBWI conference and heard Marion Dane Bauer speak. She said she, too, had grown up reading Golden Books, those grocery store aisle literary temptations. For some reason, that simple statement made me believe again that I might be able to write for children. While at that conference in Wisconsin, I was "volunteered" to be the Regional Advisor for a non-existent SCBWI chapter in Illinois. Having seen it work before, I rounded up a half dozen others from the SCBWI roster and we started a chapter in Chicago, all of us again fulfilling several leadership roles. Again, I found real fulfillment in starting critique groups, leading discussions, sharing what I'd learned and learning from others. I even had a writing group that met for years every other week at my house, half of whose members were actually publishing. We'd have champagne and cake when they signed their contracts. I'd wash the dishes after they'd all gone and wonder if it would ever happen to me. By then it had been a decade since that first luncheon in Texas and all I'd had were, at best, what we called "good" rejections. My writing group had even tried to lessen the blow by renaming them "graceful declines."

Have you ever had any of those? Somehow they make you feel grateful to be rejected. I used to think it was a bit of masochism, but now I think those encouraging words actually kept my new identity as a budding writer intact. I still could belong to this group; I could really be a writer, even if not yet recognized as one outside my tiny circle.

About that time I was asked to teach some new Writing for Children sections in my local community college's continuing education department. Why me? Only a few other writers had heard of me or of my work. Who had told them about me? It turned out that they had called one of the published members in my writer's group and she'd declined, but given them my name. Okay. I'd give it a try. What a lark it turned out to be. I knew just a bit more than my students, so that worked out well, and many of them became friends and SCBWI members, and some of them are published writers today.

What did I learn? I learned that I could teach.

I also learned from that experience and the two SCBWI chapters that I liked to start things. That led to my employment as a Licensed Lay Minister for my denomination in a new church start-up in the next suburb over, where I taught kid's classes and led adult groups, and remembered way back when I wanted to be the preacher's wife so I could do those things.

What a gratifying couple of years, fulfilling an early aspiration and defying those in the fundamentalist church of my youth who once told me that a woman would never be allowed to lead in that way. I was also not doing much writing having decided I might return to theological seminary. I did miss my characters and stories, but the thrill of the new church start and the experience of making a difference in real people's lives were seductive for a while.

Have you had a period of time like that? A time when you turned to some other potentially more fulfilling and/or successful career path? Maybe you have given up writing for a while, too. Or are you wondering today whether to give it up altogether or to continue? I cannot tell you that there are no other fulfilling pathways for you to follow. There are, and some of them pay well. But are they what you are meant to do? I think that if you are like me you might plan to meet with other writers or attend conferences to get that shot in the arm you need to keep the faith, to grab onto inspiration and courage, to remind yourself where you really belong. As gratifying as that short stint as a minister was to the child of my memory, it didn't prove to be the right thing for me. I realized it didn't fulfill the purpose I was meant to fulfill. But what was that purpose?

I turned back to my old manuscripts, began some new ones, took some classes in literary fiction, and renewed my resolve. But the biggest step was to realize that I needed to read, write, grow as a person by confronting issues through story, no matter what the outcome was, even if I never got published. Once I realized that my identity was intact only as a writer one who strives for excellence, for beauty in language, and truth in story, I think something let loose inside me. Why? Because I quit worrying about how to change those graceful declines into acceptances and just accepted what I needed to write, accepted my heart and soul stories, no matter whether any other than my writer friends ever read them. I agreed to have a small audience. I agreed to write what I knew I needed to write.

That brought me to Vermont College at forty-five to work on the MFA in Writing degree. Too old, some might say. Not me. Looking back now, I see how much I had to gain. I had learned some new things about myself, but, oh, I still had so many more to discover. For one, I fell in love with poetry and switched from fiction to poetry half way through the program. I inhaled it, dreamed it, and learned new ways of revising prose from it. Who would have thought something like that could happen after all those years of trying to find out who I was and discover where I belonged?

I learned that I was a poet and belonged at Vermont College.

Just after I graduated, my first book was accepted and I began teaching at Columbia College Chicago downtown in the loop. I also became a graduate assistant for the first residency (January 1997) of the Vermont College of Fine Arts MFA in Writing for Children and Young Adults, and soon was hired to teach in the program. My first book came out in 2000 just after my fifty-second birthday. Too old? Now I look back at the years since and all that's happened, the other books, the students I've taught whose courage and work have moved me so deeply, those who have had books published and those who are still writing, published or not, who, like me, have taken a long time to settle into this career, and I look at the Vermont College of Fine Arts campus, and this new college we have built, and I know that I have learned a few things. Now, I know that I love being a teacher, and that my true ministry, if you will, is as an advisor at VCFA where I belong, where I have an identity that is true and real and still open to whatever comes next. I know that I haven't been and am not now alone on this path. Faculty and students have joined together to write our stories, to teach each other, and to come to know and accept who we are as unique beings.

A community of writers gives me strength to continue to do my work, and it gives me new resolve to be true to my calling, to lead, to teach, to start, to build, to tell the story of the times of our lives. Most of all, it gives me the courage to write what I must write. This may not be the path to fame or riches, but it is, for me at least, the path of joy.

About fame and riches: Do you wonder what we can do about the marketplace and its fickleness?

Nothing.

Do you think there is any way to catch the next trend once we identify it and jump on it before the tail end whips round?

Maybe, but probably not.

If you want to be with a trend, you probably will have to be the one who starts it. As it happens, the *zeitgeist* does sometimes grab a few of us at the same time, but will we rely upon that kind of odd chance to give us our subjects, characters, or to determine how we write?

No. We have to write the stories we are given to write. We have to believe in them, and to believe we are ready and able to write what needs to be written.

We are writers because we have to be. If you don't have to be, then just stop. Writing is a far too hard and precarious profession to follow if you can possibly not do it. But if it has a hold on you, don't fight it. Go with it. Allow it to be what and who you are. Completely.

What do we think we are doing? Why? How do we keep going against all odds? We just do. It is our purpose in life, our duty, our joy, and our love.

Write a word. Then another. Change a word and write a new word, another, another, another. Imagine a world and build it brick by brick, word by word, a world only you can create. Birth characters only you can animate. Do this for yourself, the child you once were and, in some memory cave, still are, and for the young person who will read your stories and enter the dream of the realms you've imagined. If you have a large audience, how wonderful, how fortunate. If you have a small one, then let it be for those special few that you work so hard. If you make a little money, enjoy it, use it well. If you make a lot, share it. If you have a little fame, bask in it; if you have a lot, don't let it go to your head. Everything is fleeting. Time changes circumstances and time and circumstance change us. We follow our paths through many lives—at least, it seems that way to me as I look back upon my many lives. I love that we are all traveling this path at the same time in the history of the world and doing this work together.

Back in 2005 when I moved to Vermont, I lived alone on a hilltop near Montpelier in an empty nest. Now, I'm married, live in a cozy warm home in a cold brook hollow in the Northeast Kingdom of Vermont, and in the last couple of years have been away from home a lot with my mother and all three of my daughters in joys and crises. I love that this work still allows me to be wherever I need to be. I love that my stories and my students travel with me and my students give me courage and delight. I love that sometimes I can set the writing aside to return to the nest and care for my children and now their young ones.

Some of you may spend all your time writing; others may teach; others become editors or agents or publishers or enter any number of word-related occupations. You'll see trends come and go, publishing companies merge and close, new technologies threaten older ones, editors retire, agents die, and you'll go through the ebb and flow that is the writing life. Some of us will flare up like fireworks and spark away, some glow like a new star, some will be a steady flame, others just a pinprick of light from far away. Some of us will go through all that and more.

Much depends upon luck, but the accomplishment of your ultimate goals can also depend upon intention and direction and resolve. That's why consciously examining your objectives and processes is so important and why the Visual Art MFA students' artist statements intrigued and challenged me. Now, I want to encourage you to write your own statement, and make it a writer's statement.

Developing Your Writer's Statement

When I speak to students about theme, or "the moral of the tale," it's most often to ask them to delete overt statements in their manuscripts that come across as too-obvious lessons meant for the edification of the child. I usually go on to say that we don't have to impress preconceived ideas onto a story because if we are writing from the deepest parts of ourselves the themes of our lives will naturally come forth. But what about checking in on our deepest selves from time to time to make sure the themes that are flowing forth rather unsuspectingly are themes we want to espouse? How about checking in with our stories now and then to make sure that we aren't inadvertently "saying" something we don't intend? How about asking ourselves questions first about where we stand in relation to the large issues of life and write with an awareness of them, allowing ourselves room to change and grow over time?

More than once in my life I've been asked to participate in generating a mission statement to guide a group's course of action in the future. We decided what service we could provide and to whom, as well as what made our group and this service unique and valuable for the target audience. I think this is a good place to start, writing one's own mission statement, but I'd like to think that writers, especially those who write for young people, might take it further, more into the realm of the artist statement where

WORLDS WITHIN WORDS · 249

we consider our motivation for this work as well as our means of delivery, our craft, our techniques and skills. And, as time goes on, remember and honor the pathways that have brought us to this place in our lives. Every once in a while it might do us good to check in with that statement to see if our stories and our skills are living up to our goals and make adjustments accordingly, revising our statements over a lifetime of growth through language and story.

Now, as I near the end of my teaching career, I've started to revise my goals, making room for new goals, even remembering old hopes and dreams. I'm working on a new artist/writer's statement, one that remembers where I've been and takes into account where I want to go, what I want to do that I haven't yet accomplished, and gives me some idea of steps to take to accomplish those goals.

As I look back, I see that much of what I have done is a testimony to how much connection, affiliation, and belonging mean to me. (Ironic, I know, considering how solitary the writing life can be.) I see that I am a person who loves to observe group dynamics and facilitate growth. I understand that though I am an introvert, groups have inspired and energized me. But they have also tired me. They have required more energy than I am likely to have in the years ahead to finish the projects I've started and to begin new ones that are only in the dream stage. I have already seen my teaching life decrease from its busiest years of full time college teaching, part time VCFA advising, school visits, conference speaking, workshop leading, and working with private students. Soon enough, there will be only the occasional speaking or teaching gig to take me from home, and eventually, not even that.

What do I have left then?

Oh, the list is so long I hardly know where to start: More writing, of course, more poetry and prose, maybe some personal essays or other non-fiction. More visual art, more music making, more travel, more family time, more enjoyment of the land around me, more just being, breathing out and breathing in. More awareness of the moment, the fleeting nature of nature, of all our lives, of my life and yours. Time to hold close the love I receive, but for only a moment to savor it fully, then turning it loose, giving as much love as I can to others. Living, loving, being my authentic self as much as I possibly can. Forgiving myself for those things I already regret and making plans to leave this life as much as possible without regrets, knowing my purpose and having dedicated myself to fulfilling it.

We do this work for ourselves, and for those readers who need our stories. We allow ourselves the seemingly egotistical notion that we have something to say, something to give, because it isn't egotistical at all. It's realistic. If you don't believe you have anything to give, you are fooling yourself and shirking your responsibility to yourself and to those who are watching, waiting, listening, needing your words. We tell each other stories because story is powerful. Great wisdom can go semi-disguised in simple story. We know more than we know that we know, and we are here to share our knowledge, to make connections, to foster empathy, and to make the world we leave a better place.

You cannot do a lot about most things outside yourself, not about the fluctuations of the marketplace or the shifting stages and tastes of your readership, but you can chart your own course. Writing an artist's—or in our case, *writer's*—statement will help you do that. I hope you will develop it, revisit it from time to time, and allow yourself the freedom and joy of being your authentic self. May the authenticity you seek bring you happiness, joyful relationships, honesty of expression, fulfilling work, and a strong purposeful life in writing.

Exercise:

Developing Your Writer's Statement

1. Describe your intentions as a writer, both in story and in craft.

2. State why you write, what drives you and what keeps you going.

3. Set forth what you intend to accomplish for your reader, your writing, and yourself.

4. Attempt to state in one sentence each the themes of your stories. Compare the statements. Is there a thematic thread that runs through all of your body of work? What is it? Is this what you intend to be putting out into the world? Do you believe what your stories are saying? Do the themes reflect your deepest convictions?

CHAPTER THIRTEEN

DISCOVERING THE REAL STORY

The exercise of imagination is one of the greatest of human gifts. To be able to conjure up people, places, events, speech, thought, and emotion; to have the capability of empathy, becoming one with another at the level of soul, spirit, heart—whatever you happen to name, it is to challenge the idea of boundaries and to defy the expected in order to make real the possibility of becoming who you were meant to be.

Revision is the process of freeing the imagination. Previously I have mentioned the stages of story exploration: 1) inspirational draft, 2) discovery drafts, 3) literary fix-up final. The first draft is inspired (as if breathed into being), a thrill to experience, and there it is—your body of clay, a first draft. Next, comes molding, forming just as one might work clay, discovering through the process of intensive exploration what the shape is meant to be. Next, we enter the editing, "fix-up" stage, making sure the grammar and punctuation are correct and work the way we intend, put the clay into the kiln, and fire it into its completely transformed and finished state.

Each of these stages overlaps with the others, and, even during the fix-up stage, the imagination should still be allowed to work. In revision we don't want to go from *Wrong Word* to *New Word*, searching our brains like a thesaurus or dictionary for a better word. Instead, we move from *Wrong Word* through *Imagination* into *Image* to discover *New Word*. Little thesaurus-mind allowed, as you go from word to the non-verbal image then back to the new word for that newfound or clearer image, moving through the imagination to word.

BEWARE: This process can change you! This process is about change and self-actualization. If this sounds all too touchy-feely, don't worry, you can resist and you can write a fine story, I'm sure, sticking to the surface of things. But what I'm talking about is real change, which is a process of self-revelation. It's not easy and not everyone wants this, but if you are willing to *be* the clay, to allow your own words to change you, you'll find the deep, real stories inside you, the true themes of your life. No need to impose theme on your stories, your themes will emerge from who you are, who you are becoming.

The process works like this: *Word to Image, through clarification of Image, to New Word, and thus to New*

Self. In order to find your character's story you must be open to all that is possible within you. For instance, in spite of your distaste, you might try to write from the points of view of your antagonists. In order to enter their sensibilities you will probably have to give them some sort of humanizing or mitigating trait, a bit of reason behind the badness, or go into their hearts of darkness where you may feel distinctly uncomfortable. In either case, you will come to understand something new about your characters and something new about yourself as the creator responsible for bringing those personalities into the world. You aren't responsible for their actions, thoughts, or feelings, but because they do come out of some part of you, a part that we writers have to acknowledge *is* a part of us, you as a result revise your concept of self. To be an excellent and successful writer is not so much about making better sentences or more charmingly crafted stories, but about being open to the revision of self through the revised word.

We confront a blank page as one self and write, creating not only a story, but also the new self, capable of having written that story. We enter revision ready to re-see not only the words on the page, but also the self that considers them. You change one word and you change yourself—that is, if you are allowing the re-engagement of your imagination fully and freely, not just seeking to locate a different word. It's not about words, but about heart.

And yet, of course, the stuff of our story-making is words. Imagined stories would remain daydreams without the written word to anchor them in the world of daylight and dark. Some people may not understand why we want to expend so much time and energy "telling stories," which when I was a little girl meant lying. We may not be able to explain no matter what we say. How does a writer say to a non-writer, "I am not making up stories; I'm making myself real"? How do you tell someone that you find reality in the imaginary, or truth in the mouths of people who have never existed and never will? If we try, it's possible we will be taken for lunatics. Ah well, if art is lunacy, so be it. On the other hand, I believe art can be a path to all that is best in the human and an avenue to authenticity in the world.

"Imagination," "revision," "the making of self"—to me, one and the same. When someone says, "Use your imagination," it is an invitation to revise your vision of the world, discover the stories and themes of your life, and to dare to dream your true self into being.

PART V

GOING FORWARD

CHAPTER FOURTEEN

RISKS TO BE TAKEN; DREAMS TO BE DREAMED

(A Graduation Address)

In January 1997, the MFA in Writing for Children and Young Adults program of Vermont College of Fine Arts had its beginning with its first winter residency. January 2017 marks the program's twentieth anniversary and forty-first residency. We've definitely come of age.

Writers have come from all over this country, across the continent, and the world to study together and to find their voices in story, nonfiction, critical prose, and poetry. Our graduates today have brought their unique voices to this campus and have shared the deepest parts of themselves with their newfound, and now lifelong, friends and readers. They have taken risks and have dared to dream their dreams together.

What courage it takes to decide to follow a dream into reality!

These writers, in the process of authoring stories, have authored new lives for themselves, new storylines filled with tension and promise, sadness and joy. While I am sure they were already heroes of their own lives, they have become more fully so and more aware of the choices available to them in the future.

This past November, during the whirlwind of life that surrounded us then, one of my heroes died—Gwen Ifill, an anchor of PBS Newshour and Washington Week. In the many televised clips of her broadcasts and speeches, one stood out to me. It was Gwen (I call her that because she seems like a real friend) addressing a graduating class the spring before her death. I caught only a snippet of it, but these few words have stuck in my mind. She said to those graduates, "There are risks to be taken...." Today, I am saying that to you, too, but adding something extra:

There *are* risks to be taken, and *there are dreams to be dreamed.*

When I see you here, ready to go, I can't help but remember my own Vermont College graduation in July 1996, a day so like this one in spirit, though a good deal warmer. We had our graduation ceremony on the lawn with the green smells of summer and flowers around us, the birds singing, the sun shining, an ice cream social and champagne reception waiting for us beside the fountain. I was amazed that I'd made it through. I was proud, and a little tired, but resolved to go forward and write like my heart was on fire. In order to keep myself on a good schedule, I made plans as if I were doing a fifth semester, plans for writing, reading, even writing essays—and what happened? I floundered around trying to find a new working schedule, one that didn't have the excuse of "it's my homework" to justify it to myself and to my family.

It took some time, several months, to renegotiate with my family after the program had ended in order to make my new life work for all of us. They had been fairly patient, but, I realized later, thought we'd return to the kind of schedule we'd had before the MFA program began.

Here, I'd like to warn the friends and family members of these graduates to expect a different sort of life from now on, and urge them to be willing to help shape the course of these writers' days, weeks, months, and years in this new and wonderful profession.

As I began my work in this new "business," I tuned in whenever I heard another writer give advice. I heard (and tried) many of the following tricks:

Getting dressed and going to work at my desk as if arriving at a nine to five job;
Not getting dressed and letting my first thoughts flow;

Making a strict daily schedule, making myself stop my preferred tasks and go to the next at the appointed time;

Involving even my youngest children in my writing life;

Sharing joys and disappointments with understanding people, like a critique group;

Setting up my own deadlines by entering contests and submitting work to editors.

However, it soon became clear that I could find ways around almost any strategy I set forth. It wasn't that I didn't want to be a writer. I did. In fact, in the years prior to seeking the MFA, I even tried to quit a few times and I learned I was a writer and I'd best get on with it. The problem was I hadn't completely internalized the process. I hadn't owned it. I hadn't truly believed I could become an author. What I needed, and what I continually need to remind myself of, was a way to conceptualize what the activities of my life meant taken as a whole.

At that time I was beginning a study and practice of yoga. I was especially taken with the concept of balance. Balance in all things is essential for health, and for the integrity of life. In yoga, life activities can be divided into these three somewhat overlapping concepts:

jnana—self-transcending knowledge, which for writers might include study, reading, research, and contemplation;

karma—selfless action, which is duty, work, planning, physical exercise, domestic and professional tasks, and could include teaching or other outreach activities;

bhakti—devotion, which might include meditation, writing, discovering more truth and more story through deep revision.

None of us will ever be perfect in any of those areas or in finding a totally serene balance, so that's where the next concept comes in: *Surrendering.* Accepting what is and that the writing life is really a lot of hard work, a lot of *heart* work, and we may only be able to approximate on paper what our heads and hearts know and understand. But we must try and to do this we have to take some risks.

You must:

Accept that the process is the process and will likely have to be explored anew for each new project;

Be brave when you see how much of yourself you must bring to the work;

Be willing to go deeper into yourself, to discover more about the emotional life of humans, and therefore, your characters;

Not get frustrated when this takes more time than you think it should;

Be patient with yourself and your characters—and your family (and family, be patient with your writer).

But in this work there is great Joy in:

The exhilaration of finding the right ending (or the right beginning);
Knowing that you've challenged yourself in ways no one else will ever know;
Learning something about life from your own writing that you didn't know, or didn't know you knew;
Hearing an editor say, "I want to buy this";
Seeing the real live published piece for the first time;
Hearing a young person say, "I want to read this";
Realizing, "Hey, I'm not an imposter after all";
Talking to people about writing and books;
Reading your work to an attentive audience;
Seeing in their faces your story come to life;
Helping someone else make more sense out of life;
Knowing you have given something of your own spirit to the world in a way that might make life a bit easier for someone else.

Or perhaps, like what happened to me, when one of my fellow students read one of my manuscripts, you'll have someone tell you that your story has helped her lay down a lifelong burden and desire for revenge, which has finally allowed her to weep over something horrible done to her long ago—and you'll realize that all those years of study and writing might have been for just that moment in that one life. And you'll know it was worth it, even if that book never gets published.

An editor once told me stories should save lives or change the world—or else what was the point? My stories may or may not do that for someone else, but my writing has saved my own life and changed my own world, and for that, I'll always be grateful and astonished.

Entering a new story with all your resources engaged and with your heart open to breaking is a risk. The work itself will change you. If it is published, it might encounter negativity. You might even be personally criticized. If it isn't published, you have to know that you have grown as a person and a writer for having written it.

What a mystery life is. I started out thinking the end product would be printed words on paper and I found that, instead, it was a changed me, and, when I am lucky, a change in my readers.

Why do you write? What is the story you need to tell yourself? Even the lightest, funniest stories can come from deep places inside us that we need to make contact with to understand our own existence. That's what makes even the most fantastic story true and writing it a risk worth taking.

What is your true story? Finding it, living in it, and giving it to others is a great joy.

Another joy for me has been this experience, here at Vermont College of Fine Arts, our work together for so much more beyond our own dreams of glory. It's a joy for me to see these graduates today, ready to explode into the world of writing, publishing, reviewing, teaching, and sharing children's literature. What a thrill it is to know that we have been making a difference in the field of writing for young people for two decades now, and that we will continue that good work for many more to come. What a proud and important field writing for children and young adults is. What could be more fun and of more use than a good book in the hands of a child ready, eager, and, perhaps, in need of a good bedtime story? At this time in our history as a country, what a great gift to give your readers—a place to go to rest, to learn, to laugh, to cry, to become heroes in their own lives, and to begin to imagine their actions in the world as adults.

Do you remember a time when you began to grow toward adulthood through reading? Here's one of my memories taken from a personal essay I wrote many years ago:

Our home at 2025 Sabine Pass in Beaumont, Texas, was just an ordinary trailer park with peppermint carnations growing in tractor tires cut into decorative points and painted white, a place much like all the others I lived in during my elementary school years. Except it comes into my dreams and in my dreams I live in all the trailers, I'm all the families, and I never know what we'll do to each other next.

Sometimes I sit in the lawn chairs and speak, "Good evenin'," or "Mornin'," and pick my flowers for a vase in my big tilted front picture window. Sometimes I yell at my kids or beat my wife, then I am the wife who runs in my slip with a torn strap, knocking on doors. Do you have a phone, call me the police, he has a butcher knife. Then I'm the one who doesn't have a phone and I just shut the door and peek to see where I go next. Not to the owners who have a phone, no I don't want them to know.

Then I am the owners and I'm not afraid of my big dog. He sits and I pat him. I'm safe. And I don't need a butcher knife either. I have a phone and sensible shoes and people who pay rent and smile so they can stay in this world I own.

Then I hear the owner call MY name over the P.A. system: Darrow, telephone, Sharon Darrow." I hope it's not my teacher calling and that she can't hear the echoing crackle of my summons running through the air flowing from all the speakers all over the park. I am my mom saying, "Yes, you have to go answer." Go past the chain link gate, past the huge teeth, up into the glassed-in porch to hold the cold black phone to my ear. I talk to my teacher and wonder if the words are pouring out the speakers, whirling past the chain link. And the children hear my voice and the old people hear my voice and those in the metal huts hear it and the nuns and all around to Charlie's store and down under the palm trees back to school and my teacher hears it.

I'm all those people in my world, but never my teacher. I dream all those lives, but I never dream hers.

There on Sabine Pass, now widened and called Martin Luther King Boulevard, when my family moved to still-segregated Beaumont, Texas from West Virginia, where all the kids no matter their skin color went to school together, my mother walked with my sister and me past the chain link fence that divided the white and black sections of town to where the white kids went to school. Our school, Pennsylvania Elementary, a white-painted brick building, old and bright, had a basement cafeteria where our teachers sat with us and taught us table manners, and then back in the classroom they read us a chapter a day from wonderful storybooks.

One day on a fifth grade field trip, we took the city bus downtown to Terrell Library, an old building with creaky wooden floors, narrow winding staircases, and the Hardy Boys, Nancy Drew, and Betty Cavanna high up in the small children's room shelves. I wondered what kind of fantastic person an author might be, and no, it never occurred to me that I might become one.

Down in the basement, when we took our bathroom break before leaving, our whole class had to line up to use the facilities and water fountain labeled "Whites Only," while the ones marked "Colored" stood empty. Later at Walgreens, we sat in booths and along the lunch counter and blew the soda straw wrappers into each other's faces.

Hanging on the wall behind the malted milk mixer, a sign said, "We reserve the right to refuse service to anyone," but, I realized then, it didn't really mean that at all—it meant "Whites Only," just like the signs in the library.

Earlier in my life I had read those signs and tried to understand why there was an invisible line dividing the people in my world, and how it was that one's birth, a stroke of happenstance, had put some of us on one side with more privileges and others on the opposite side with fewer. That invisible and imaginary line, but nonetheless a real and effective divider, attempted to justify denying half of the people around me some of the simplest and basic privileges I enjoyed. The older I got and with a year of integrated education in West Virginia, I began to grasp what that line was made of: fear, ignorance, and hate. That day at the library, beyond the glimpse into the world of books to be read and enjoyed, I encountered those signs in a different way and saw them for what they were. I also remember feeling helpless to do anything about it because I was also learning that people I respected accepted these divisions as normal, as "that's just the way it is."

The next school year, my sixth grade classroom had its own library. In a U-shaped alcove in the back corner, our teacher had filled the shelves with books. Perfect books for me at that time in my life, books about girls, some characters in Lois Lenski's books who talked like me, and in others young heroines who lived in dramatic, dangerous, and important times: *Little Maid of Plymouth Rock,*

Little Maid of Valley Forge, Little Maid of Gettysburg. I wondered what it would be like to live in a time when what I did might make a difference to my country and to my world. Though a fantasy beyond my aspirations, I wondered if I would have been the kind of girl I read about who would take risks and dream dreams for the greater good of her world. I hoped somehow I would be. Still, all I managed to do right then was live deep in the confusion of a divided culture.

Many years later, after I'd surprised myself and started teaching in this MFA program and at a college in the Chicago loop, my picture book biography of Mary Shelley was chosen to be a part of Chicago's Public Library's Frankenstein exhibit programming. (Yes, I'd surprised myself by becoming an author, too.) I was asked to speak to librarians and some Chicago Public School students whose teachers would bring them downtown for a field trip to the library. I had to stop and remember my first trip to visit a real library there in Beaumont and my first glimpse of a private library in my sixth grade classroom. While preparing my talk and remembering those libraries, I sat looking at the floor-to-ceiling shelves that covered one wall of my Victorian apartment in Chicago and pondered what it means to HAVE a library, to be able to hold the books I love in my hands whenever I want. To read them, loan them, give them away. And there, tucked in alongside all those other wonderful books stood my own stories, the books I had written. There I sat in the life I had not even dared to dream. The life of being a teacher, and of being an author.

How could this be? How could *that* girl get *here*? She wasn't wise or heroic, hadn't made history, but somehow, one day, she held a library book in her hand and made a connection between her life and the lives of the people she read about in books and those she saw around her. She listened to the voices she'd heard all her life and knew they deserved to be heard, whether they were noble or foolish, brave or scared, hopeful or beaten down. She—and they—somehow found their voices.

Back in the days I've told you about I couldn't dream a life like my teachers'. But those teachers, the librarians I met, and those authors I'd never met dreamed a life for me. They put books in my hands. And into my heart. I went inside the *Heart of Darkness*, *Far from the Madding Crowd*, in the best of times and the worst of times, through *The Dark Labyrinth*. I was there when *Their Eyes were Watching God*. Now, I can dream dreams beyond the possibilities of my childhood—and the childhood of this nation.

I didn't realize then in those early days of the Civil Rights movement that we were in the midst of a decades-long revolution in our country or that it would get much worse before it got any better. I didn't realize that real forces worked against what I believed were my nation's core values of love, peace, and brotherhood/sisterhood. But one day I did realize that I, too, would have to find a way to become a patriot by hoping, praying, and working to make a better world in the future. Most children in the America of today don't realize the steep precipice upon which their lives rest. But when they do, they will need us—the librarians, readers, guides, teachers—and writers. We will put books in their hands and nourish the dreams in their hearts.

What does that mean exactly? How can we make sure that all children have the chance I had even if they weren't born on the privileged side of our society's many dividing lines? Except for the socioeconomic situation I grew up in, I was in all other aspects among the most privileged people anywhere, not just in my country, but in the whole world. Now, we have to do what was done for me—and probably for you—through books and story, and make sure that all people's stories get told and get heard and read. We have to combat discrimination and racism with any weapons we writers have in order to make sure we have representation for all our diverse children between the covers of the books they read, and that there is a welcoming place for their myriad stories.

Why? Because we have to. Even if there are risks to be taken. Because that's what we are here for. Here. Now. To save lives and change the world. To dream dreams, even for those who haven't dared to dream for themselves. To put books in the hands of those who need our stories and to use our unique voices to speak for those who have no voice.

There is a crisis of division in our land, a ever-widening difference in the definition of values and a difference of opinion about things of the spirit. We may not all have the same definitions for the words in what the New Testament calls the first commandment: "Love the Lord your God with all your heart, mind, and soul." But I just bet you we all can understand the second, like unto it: "Love your neighbor as yourself."

Because of books and the life experiences they have enlightened for me, I've learned that I am my neighbor and my neighbor is me. Rather than drawing dividing lines and erecting chain link fences between us, it's time to break the chains that divide us and discover the links that unite us, for we are all essential and interlocking pieces of the great puzzle of life.

There are risks to be taken; there are dreams to be dreamed: let this be your call to action. Dear writers, yours is a fine and noble task.

NOTES ON THE ESSAYS

The Writing Life

1. The Clothesline: Place and Identity

2. Voice, Inspiration and Meaning

Bly, Carol. *Beyond the Writers' Workshop: New Ways to Write Creative Nonfiction.* New York: Anchor, 2001.

Darrow, Sharon. Illus. Kathryn Brown. *Old Thunder and Miss Raney.* New York: Dorling Kindersley, 2000.

---. *The Painters of Lexieville.* Cambridge: Candlewick, 2003.

---. Illus. Angela Barrett. *Through the Tempests Dark and Wild: A Story of Mary Shelley, Creator of Frankenstein.* Cambridge: Candlewick, 2003.

---. *Trash.* Cambridge: Candlewick, 2006.

Hawthorne, Alice (Septimus Winner). "Whispering Hope." Public Domain, 1868.

3. Portals and Negative Space

Keats, John, ed. Robert Gittings. *Letters of John Keats.* London: Oxford U.P., 1992.

The Craft and the Art

4. Characterization: Choosing Point of View

Bauer, Marion Dane. *Runt.* New York: Clarion, 2002.

Fletcher, Susan. *Shadow Spinner.* New York: Aladdin, 1998.

Wynne-Jones, Tim. *Stephen Fair*. Harper Trophy, 2000.

5. Emotion and Revision: The "Emotional Core"

Wilcox, Helen [et. al.], eds. *The Body and the Text: Helene Cixous—Reading and Teaching*. New York: St. Martin's, 1990.

Garcia Lorca, Federico. "The Duende: Theory and Divertissement," 1933. Ben Belitt translation, 1955.

Taylor, Jill Bolte. "Paul Ekman." Time Magazine, Thursday, April 30, 2009.

Welty, Eudora. *The Eye of the Story*. New York: Vintage, 1979.

6. Two Sides of the Same Coin: The Character's Emotional Journey and The Plot

Hawes, Louise. *Black Pearls*. Boston: Houghton Mifflin, 2008.

Lynch, Chris. *Freewill*. New York: Harper Collins, 2001.

Mazer, Norma Fox. *Good Night, Maman*. San Diego: Harcourt Brace, 1999.

7. The Plot of the Sentence: Some Tactics of Syntax

James, Henry. *The Golden Bowl*. New York: Oxford U.P., 2009.

8. Poetry: "A Messy Business"

Cohen, Patricia. "W. S. Merwin to be Named Poet Laureate." New York Times, June 30, 2010.

Dobyns, Stephen. *Best Words, Best Order*. 2nd Ed. London: Palgrave Macmillan, 2003.

---. *Next Word, Better Word: The Craft of Writing Poetry.* London: Palgrave Macmillan, 2011.

Kunitz, Stanley, and Genine Lentine. *The Wild Braid: A Poet Reflects on a Century in the Garden.* New York: W. W. Norton, 2007.

Young, Dean. *The Art of Recklessness: Poetry as Assertive Force and Contradiction.* Minneapolis: Graywolf Press, 2010.

The Teaching Writer

9. *Teaching: The Process Approach to Writing*

Atwell, Nancy. *In the Middle: New Understandings about Writing, Reading, and Learning.* 2nd Ed. Portsmouth, NH: Heinemann, 1998.

---. *Side by Side: Essays on Teaching to Learn.* Portsmouth, NH: Heinemann, 1991.

Coman, Carolyn. "Re: Teaching Writing." Email received by Sharon Darrow.

Elbow, Peter. *Embracing Contraries: Explorations in Learning and Teaching.* New York: Oxford U.P., 1986.

Freire, Paolo. *Pedagogy of the Oppressed.* New York: Continuum, 1997.

---. *Teachers as Cultural Workers: Letters to Those Who Dare Teach.* Boulder, CO: Westview, 1998.

Howard, Ellen. "Re: Teaching Writing." Email received by Sharon Darrow.

Keats, John, ed. Robert Gittings. *Letters of John Keats.* London: Oxford U.P., 1992.

Machado, Antonio. "Proverbios y cantares." *Campos de Castilla*. 1912.

Transtromer, Tomas. "At Funchal." *The Half-finished Heaven: The Best Poems of Tomas Transtromer*. 2nd Ed. Minneapolis: Graywolf, 2001.

10. The Writing and Teaching Life

Atwell, Nancy. *In the Middle: New Understandings about Writing, Reading, and Learning*. 2nd Ed. Portsmouth, NH: Heinemann, 1998.

---. *Side by Side: Essays on Teaching to Learn*. Portsmouth, NH: Heinemann, 1991.

Elbow, Peter. *Embracing Contraries: Explorations in Learning and Teaching*. New York: Oxford U.P., 1986.

Freire, Paolo. *Pedagogy of the Oppressed*. New York: Continuum, 1997.

11. "Write at Your Own Risk" Excerpts & Other Short Pieces

Bukowski, Charles. *Love Is a Dog From Hell: Poems 1974-1977*. Santa Rosa: Black Sparrow Press. 1977.

Elbow, Peter. *Embracing Contraries: Explorations in Learning and Teaching*. New York: Oxford U.P., 1986.

Freire, Paolo. *Pedagogy of the Oppressed*. New York: Continuum, 1997.

Longfellow, Henry Wadsworth. "Introduction to Evangeline: A Tale of Acadie." 1847. Public Domain.

McMillan, Terry. *Waiting to Exhale*. New York: Viking Press. 1992.

Mencken, H.L. *A Little Book in C Major*, 1916.

Shakespeare, William. "Sonnet 116," 1609.

Welty, Eudora. *The Eye of the Story.* New York: Vintage, 1979. Print.

Writeatyourownrisk.com (Booth, Darrow, Larios Wynne-Jones,)

Imagination, Revision, and Self-Making
12. What Do You Think You Are Doing?
13. Discovering the Real Story

Going Forward
14. Risks to be Taken; Dreams to be Dreamed (A Graduation Address)

Ifill, Gwen. PBSNewhour. Vermont Public Television. Nov. 15, 2016.

ABOUT THE AUTHOR

Sharon Darrow has taught in the MFA in Writing for Children and Young Adults, Vermont College of Fine Arts, since 1997, as well as the English Department of Columbia College Chicago, and in school visits, conferences, and retreats. She is the author of *Old Thunder and Miss Raney* (art by Kathryn Brown), finalist for Western Writers of America Spur Award; *Yafi's Family* (co-author Linda Pettit, art by Jan Spivey Gilchrist), winner of Skipping Stones and Mom's Choice Awards; *Through the Tempests Dark and Wild: A Story of Mary Shelley, Creator of Frankenstein* (art by Angela Barrett), a Junior Library Guild selection; a novel, *The Painters of Lexieville*, named to KLIATT's Editors' Choice—Best of the Year YA Fiction list and winner of the Oklahoma Book Award; and a long narrative in poems, *TRASH*, Junior Library Guild selection and a finalist for the Oklahoma Book Award. Her poetry for young people has been included in *Home to Me: Poems Across America,* edited by Lee Bennett Hopkins and her poems, short stories, interviews, and personal essays for adults have appeared in literary journals *Rhino, Folio, Whetstone, ACM (Another Chicago Magazine), Columbia Poetry Review, Great River Review, Other Voices, The Writer's Chronicle,* and in the anthology, *In the Middle of the Middle West*, edited by Becky Bradway.

She was born in Oklahoma, raised in Texas, Mississippi, Kentucky, West Virginia, Arkansas, Louisiana, and lived much of her adult life in the Chicago area. She now lives in the Northeast Kingdom of Vermont.

www.ingramcontent.com/pod-product-compliance
Lightning Source LLC
Chambersburg PA
CBHW020609300426
44113CB00007B/568